The
Pittsburgh
Anthology

Eric Boyd

This book brought to you in part by the generous support
of the Carnegie Museum of Art, Pittsburgh, Pennsylvania.

Printed in Pennsylvania

First Printing, 2015

ISBN-13: 978-0-9859441-9-3

Belt Publishing
http://www.beltmag.com

Book design by Haley Stone
Cover design by Haley Stone
Cover photograph by Dave DiCello

Also by
Belt Publishing

The Youngstown Anthology
A Detroit Anthology
The Cincinnati Anthology
The Cleveland Anthology

Table of Contents

Introduction   12

From the Diaspora   16
Bethany Lang

Pittsburgh Sandlots   19
Jody DiPerna

Banjos on the North Side   27
Nico Chiodi

Is Pittsburgh America's Most Livable City?   30
Sean Posey

Steel City Fandom   36
Brendan Hykes

Chasing the Illusion   44
Cody McDevitt

Hour of Love   51
Jess Craig

Homestead Triptych   57
Rachel Wilkinson

The Heart of Saturday Night   61
Kyle Mimnaugh

Time Capsule, 2005   65
Robert Yune

The T to Nowhere   68
J.J. Lendl

Retraced Route   74
Adam Dupaski

The Lonesome Passing of Jay Paulson   83
Andy Kohler

The Mt. Washington Monument   88
Melanie Cox McCluskey

Rust Belt Heroin Chic   94
Ben Gwin

Rebecca Morgan Paintings   105

Robert Qualters Paintings   113

Stoplight   121
Amy Jo Burns

Look, Decrease   126
Eric Boyd

LaToya Ruby Frazier Photographs   133

The Bottoms   144
Matthew Newton

The Missing Made Visible: In the Footsteps of Teenie Harris   152
Yona Harvey

Bright Pittsburgh Morning   156
Maricio Kilwein Guevara

The Altar Boy   157
Maricio Kilwein Guevara

A Middle Aged Student's Guide to Social Work   158
Dave Newman

Brownfields   172
John Lawson

At Pegasus   173
Terrance Hayes

I'm Into Leather   175
Lori Jakiela

Won't You Be My Neighbor?   185
Rachel Mabe

Equity   191
Michael Gerhard Martin

Picksburgh Sampler–Furill   195
Ann Curran

The Pittsburgh Poem Is   196
Ann Curran

Lost City   198
Lisa Toboz

Rebirth of the Hollywood Lanes   205
Kevin Tasker

The River Underneath the City   208
Scott Silsbe

I'm Still a Jagov But I Love It   209
Scott Silsbe

Bob Perkoski Photographs   210

A Poem Written for the Aviary at a Time of its Possible Closing   215
Robert Gibb

Steelworkers' Lockers, Pittsburgh History Center   217
Robert Gibb

The Hall of Architecture   218
Robert Gibb

Steel Engravings   219
Robert Gibb

from The Employments of Time in the Homestead   221
Robert Gibb

Enclave (for Jimmy Cvetic)   223
Matthew Plumb

Shopping is Your Warholian Duty   224
Arielle Teer

Contributors   228

Editor's Acknowledgements   235

The Pittsburgh Anthology

Introduction

Pittsburgh is changing. I don't know if it's for the better or for the worse. I once worked for the USW...as a camera-man for their secretly-funded protest of Chinese goods. I worked on top of West Mifflin's great Slag Mountain...at the local Wal-Mart. I even worked in Homestead, but long after the mills there had been paved over.

What's always been odd is how much history was a part of those situations. Little remnants of the old steel industry are littered across the area. A smokestack here, a ladle rail-car there. But while the shadow of this town's past is long, it's not inescapable. Braddock and Clairton still have mills, but it's possible to meet people there who have nothing to do with the steel industry, and whose families never did. Pittsburgh's moved on. It's had to. It's moved on to new money — to hipsters, craft beer, technology. Roads and bridges are being fitted with bike lanes. The Southside's Carson Street is getting more and more upscale bars and hookah shops. The economic wounds of the city seem to be stabilizing, though it's hard to know exactly at what cost.

This collection of essays and art will attempt to examine modern-day Pittsburgh from every angle. My hope is that it will be surprising, elusive, and different. For instance, our very first piece isn't set in Pittsburgh; instead, in a nod to the all-too-familiar story of Pittsburghers who aren't here anymore, Bethany Lang will describe how hard it is to go on a date when you're away from the town you love.

Surprises like that were important to me. This entire book is filled with curveballs. And, on that note I knew that, in editing this first Belt anthology on the Burgh, I'd want to avoid sports at almost any cost. Once, at a diner in New York, a friend of mine introduced me, saying, "This is Eric, he's from Pittsburgh." The waiter at the diner looked at me, made two fists, and grinned: "STEEELERRRS!"

In many of these pieces it's impossible to say if a good thing is happening in a bad place, or a bad thing in a good one. It's a fine introduction to our city of proud contradictions.

So everyone knows all of that; instead, one of the book's early pieces, by Jody Diperna, takes a look at some of the teams people may not be as familiar with. Elswhere, Nico Chiodi — at 15, the book's youngest contributor — tells us about the Pittsburgh Banjo Club, popular among those who know of it, but a hidden gem for most. Sean Posey asks what exactly makes Pittsburgh this country's "Most Liveable City" and Brendan Hykes attends a number of the various conventions that have become so popular here. Cody Mcdevitt examines the pros and cons of Western PA's casinos, and Jess Craig shows us all of the love and friendship that surrounds the Allegheny County Jail. Finally, Rachel Wilkinson travels through the centuries that took Homestead from an American industrial giant to a gentrified big-box shopping plaza. In many of these pieces it's impossible to say if a good thing is happening in a bad place, or a bad thing in a good one. It's a fine introduction to our city of proud contradictions.

Throughout the editing process I kept in mind one goal: to show off Pittsburgh stories told by Pittsburghers, old and new. Often I would tell writers, "Be more conversational. Add more dialogue. Give me anecdotes and put me there."

It's a well-known fact is that Pittsburgh has the most bars, per capita, in America (12 for every 10,000 residents). The deeper you go into this book, the more I want that environment to set in. I want you to see the authors on the stools next to you. At the bar is a pretty bad bartender — has too many regulars and pours too heavily for them — but the owner can't do nothing about it because the cherry machine pays out illegally and that could be big trouble if anyone ever said anything. Behind you there's someone trying to figure out the jukebox and next to them a man's laid his quarters down on the pool table for dibs on the next game. You're pulling at your beer, and one of the authors turns to you and says, "Hey, you think you heard it all? Lemme tell ya about this…"

Throughout this book, they'll tell you. From triumph to heartbreak they'll share unforgettable stories and images. Kyle Mimnaugh, a certified film nut, will teach you to appreciate the incredible number of movie theatres in this region. Ben Gwin will take a hard look at the heroin problem that's become a regional epidemic, and it's personal impact on the ones he's loved. (In fact, over the night of this writing, ten people were reported for overdoses across the city. One died. Every year, it seems, a new batch of bad stuff enters the market here.)

Art and photography show up, as beautiful as it is unexpected; every visual in this book is striking and dreamlike. To have folks like Robert Qualters, Rebecca Morgan, and LaToya Ruby Frazier in one book is a feast you won't soon forget.

Reflections on the past take root in the present as Matthew Newton shows the personal toll of this region's high military enrollment (1 out of 12 citizens in Southwestern PA is involved with the military — over a quarter of a million veteran families — making it one of the most concentrated areas in America). Yona Harvey gazes into a photograph from the city's 1968 race riots and, in turn, looks at what the city is today. Amy Jo Burns, author of the mesmerizing Cinderland, continues to explore how her hometown — the place she most loved — was the place she most wanted to leave. Terrance Hayes reads a poem about a wondrous alternative dance club that isn't there anymore. In an aptly named piece, Dave Newman takes you through "A Middle-Aged Student's Guide to Social Work" (originally published here at Belt). And, greedy as I am, I even take a look at how the medical community in Pittsburgh provides opportunities for some of the more financially desperate residents here, myself included. We'll end the book, appropriately, with a call to enjoy some modern art and go shopping (hopefully for more copies of this book, eh? Friends, family, turnpike attendants … they'd all like one. Please folks, we need the money).

The writers and artists in this collection will go through the history of Pittsburgh to figure out why it is how it is today. Everyone in this book is talking about the city, the things surrounding it; all of the pieces have been created with experience, intimacy, and personality. This book, I hope, will speak to you, not at you.

Because we all know this city is changing. We're just not exactly sure what that means.

So sit down and we'll figure it out together. This round's on us.

Eric Boyd
Pittsburgh, Pennsylvania

From the Diaspora

Bethany Lang

I *went on a first date yesterday.* Inevitably, the fact that I am from Pittsburgh came up in conversation very quickly. I say inevitably not because where you're from is typical first date small talk (though it is), but because Pittsburghers take an almost perverse delight in telling people and talking about where they are from. This is not the same type of "I love my hometown" kind of stuff that most people spout off when they meet someone new. I always knew that Pittsburghers' love of talking about Pittsburgh very nearly verged on the suspicious and creepy, but my date was the first person to confirm this to me.

"Oh, you're from Pittsburgh," he rather suspiciously intoned.

"You sound concerned," I replied.

"I've only known one other person from Pittsburgh. Her name was Rebecca, but we called her 'Pittsburgh my cats Rebecca.' Pittsburgh was always the first thing she talked about. "'This town doesn't have X. Pittsburgh does. You know what this town needs? This thing they have in Pittsburgh.'"

"Did you know Michael Keaton is from Pittsburgh? Jeff Goldblum?" I brightly interjected. He raised his eyebrows. I had proved his point.

I left Pittsburgh when I was 17 to go to college in Chicago, where I still live today. I left in 2004. The city was beginning its slow, steady incline to hipness, prosperity, and an abundance of medical facilities owned by several warring health care conglomerates. But in 2004, the idea of Pittsburgh becoming a hip place that people moved to from Portland still seemed pretty unimaginable. I was born in 1986, so my formative years there were after the shock of the steel industry's departure, but before things really turned around.

In my childhood memories, Pittsburgh is eternally covered in cold, grey drizzle. (Did you know that Pittsburgh is the fourth-cloudiest city in the country?) Rick Sebak narrates everything, with a low backdrop of whatever '50s or '60s golden oldie from 3WS I have stuck in my head (The Supremes' "I Hear a Symphony" is a regular standard). On the best Saturday mornings, there is a trip to the Strip, where we eat homemade pepperoni rolls and buy cheap toys like magnetic Chinese checkers. On Sundays, there are chipped ham BBQ sandwiches and Myron Cope "hmm-haww-ing" and Bill Hilgrove providing the inimitable play-by-play.

There is much childish maligning of Cleveland (T-shirts emblazoned with a highway sign marking 142 miles to Pittsburgh, subtitled "the only sign of life in Cleveland"), and later, Baltimore. There is my grandmother's Pittsburgh accent, "worsh," "crick," "yinz," and all. There are church carnivals on hot summer nights with the world's best Polish food. There are the glorious Pirates led by Jim Leyland, quickly followed by the sad-sack Pirates who did not have a winning season until I had lived in Chicago for close to 10 years. There is the eternal optimism of Kennywood Day: I have friends to go with this year, it will be warm enough to ride the water rides, I will eat all of the Potato Patch cheese fries, I will not get scared on Noah's Ark.

There are the skeletons of steel mills, like the one where my father worked every summer in college to pay for his education and my grandfather was an engineer. There are echoes of Europe everywhere, from exquisite Italian food on every corner to the Lithuanian dancers to the Hills, Polish and Squirrel. There is the first time that I trudged up the stairs to Jerry's Records to find heaven in vinyl, and my first slice of pie at Gullifty's. There is the ubiquity of the Gateway Clipper fleet, from Mother's Day brunches, to the Good Ship Lollipop, to prom on the Majestic.

But my most enduring memories of Pittsburgh are of its views. When I first moved to Chicago, I spent a good six months harboring some vague suspicion that there was a Mt. Washington-style lookout somewhere that would bring the whole city into view. I truly could not believe—whether for logical or purely emotional reasons—that every city did not have a place to take the entire city in in one greedy view. Mt. Washington is great, and so is the slow drop from the Incline, but then there is the view from the Liberty Tunnels.

Bursting forth into the city from the Liberty Tunnels is one of life's great joys, because it truly does feel like bursting. You don't emerge slowly or hesitantly; you are packed into a pneumatic tube, pressurized at a tremendous rate until you explode from a dark, dingy tunnel into a dark, gorgeous city with hills and rivers and bridges on the periphery, slows exits to the North and South Hills.

Like anyone born and raised in the same place, I have a lot of memories of Pittsburgh. All of us in the Pittsburgh diaspora do. Some of us are going back; others prefer to stay where they are but savor the atmosphere of home at one of the country's hundreds of Steelers bars. All of us, however, have an unwavering commitment to talking about Pittsburgh as much as humanly possible and sharing the yinzer gospel.

Did you know the polio vaccine was invented in Pittsburgh?

Pittsburgh Sandlots

Jody DiPerna

O*n a frigid night in March 2008,* I stood on a high school football field on the South Side in a slashing rain watching the Pittsburgh Passion women's full-contact football team practice. Night practice was a thrice-weekly thing to accommodate the regular jobs of the players and coaches. It was exhausting to watch—I couldn't imagine what it was like for the players who had put in a full work day before practicing until 10:00, some with long drives back home afterwards.

I was chasing a story about the Passion, a team preparing to defend their undefeated 2007 championship season; while at work on the story, people asked lots of stupid questions about women's football, but the question I came back to over and over and over was, why? Why do it when you're not being paid? When it's hard and you're tired? And you might get injured? Some people think you're nuts for even trying. Why do it? Why show up, night after night, to play football?

Like many great athletes, it was hard for Passion QB Lisa Horton to explain how she played so beautifully and why she worked so hard at her craft. It was just in her, I suppose—both the talent and the work ethic. It showed on the field. In 2014, Horton became the first woman to throw for more than 10,000 yards in a career. But if Horton couldn't fully articulate her relationship to the sport, one of the Passion players with whom I became closest was tight end Kate Sullivan and Sully was blessed with the gift of gab. A story she told me when the season was over really got to the heart of the why, without explicitly answering the question. "The first football injury I had, I had a sprained ankle. I sprained it really bad. I can remember sitting on this table, and the doc pulls out the x-ray film and he's looking at it, he's touching all the little metatarsal bones and looks at me and says, 'Do you really have to do this? Why can't you just play some pick up? Some flag football in the park on Saturday?' I was like, 'Excuse me?' So he said, 'I don't understand why you and your friends can't just go play flag in the park on Saturday.' I could not even fathom what he was saying. This is a lot different than flag. This is not two-hand touch. This isn't freeze-tag.... It's not summer camp. I could not get over that his solution was, just, 'Why don't you just stop and get your friends and play in the park.' I thought, I hate you. I will never see you again. I didn't. I did not ever see him again."

Now and again the national sports media drop by Pittsburgh and inserts the well-trod term 'blue collar' into their stories, as though simply saying working class explains it all. Aside from the fact that it's tired, it doesn't get to the heart of what Sully told me about playing, or what I witnessed watching her team practice, or frankly, how the down-at-the-heel mill town where I grew up puffed out with pride when the Steelers won four Super Bowls in the 1970s.

The connection between the region and the sport is an actual thing. It is real and even the most hackneyed talking head can feel it. But though it is best known through the Steelers, it's bigger than just one team. There is an interconnectivity through all the sports and neighborhoods that shape the city I call home. It is a hardy, complex relationship and it is one which did not happen in one generation, monochromatically, or exclusive to one gender.

Since that freezing night of Passion practice at Cupples Field, I've been chasing down every rabbit hole and across every sandlot I could find to piece together the Pittsburgh sports collective soul for I, too, believe in the Western Pennsylvania church of football, even when I don't want to.

§

Long before the NFL became the year-round money making behemoth it is in the 21st century, it was a sport of extremes, played either on exclusive college campuses or on rugged, homely sandlots in places like Pittsburgh, Canton and Pottsville. The Hope-Harveys were one of those sandlot teams playing on Pittsburgh's North Side. Back then, professional football was considered not simply coarse, but a degraded, disreputable form of the game. Art Rooney played for and then purchased the Hope-Harveys, then renamed them the Pirates after the city's baseball team (a few years after that, they became the Steelers).

At the same time that Rooney's football team was scraping along, the Pittsburgh Crawfords baseball team was becoming one of the finest black teams in the nation showcasing such all-time greats as Oscar Charleston, Judy Johnson, Cool Papa Bell, Buck Leonard, Josh Gibson and Satchel Paige. Of course, the Crawfords had their own hurdles to clear, which were legion.

There were various amalgamations of black teams and leagues, multiple iterations constituting what we now think of as "the Negro Leagues," with associations and rival leagues starting and folding and changing shape. One of the most enduring teams was another black Pittsburgh team, Josh Gibson's first team, the Homestead Grays. The Grays were founded in 1912 and weathered all storms for 38 seasons.

The Grays weathered some financial storms and struggled to keep up with the Crawfords, but were in much better shape than many teams. Money issues abounded throughout all the leagues. Some teams were financially viable, like Kansas City's Monarchs and the Crawfords, but many others struggled to meet payroll on a game-to-game basis. Additionally, the lack of a unified, cohesive, central infrastructure made it harder to track teams, players, and stats; the *Pittsburgh Courier*, one of the best and most well-respected black papers in the nation, all but begged for teams to report scores and stats, often to little avail.

Like many Negro League baseball teams, Rooney's football team wasn't always financially solvent, either. In addition to payroll concerns, one of the big challenges facing the football Pirates was simply logistical: where could they play their games? Rooney needed a central, accessible spot, one that would be an easy draw for fans. Hard as it is to imagine today, back in the 1920s and 1930s, nobody wanted professional football played on their fields. Pittsburgh's major league baseball franchise, the Pirates, could have rented Forbes Field to the football Pirates, but they didn't want to damage their grass, so they declined. And the University of Pittsburgh certainly didn't want Rooney's sandlot roughians sullying their pristine amateur field with their plebeian, monetized sport. In 1932, the year before his team joined the ranks of the NFL, Rooney turned to another outsider to solve the location dilemma.

Like Rooney's football team, black baseball teams typically rented facilities from white teams whose schedules (and whims) they had to work around. Of course, in the instance of black teams, there was usually a layer of noxious racism to contend with, as well. Often players were forbidden from using locker rooms and, in much of the country, African American fans had to sit in segregated seating in the park. In some southern ballparks, that area was penned in by chicken-wire.

Gus Greenlee, owner of the Crawfords, had the finances to do things differently, in part because of his successful nightclub, the Crawford Grill, and also through his book-making enterprises. He decided to build his own stadium, one where his team could use all the facilities, schedule games as he pleased and, not least of all, permit their fans to sit wherever they liked. Greenlee settled on a spot just a few blocks from his nightclub in Pittsburgh's Hill District, just 'the Hill' to locals. It took all manner of wheeling and dealing to obtain the land and get appropriate zoning permits in place; construction took over six months time, $100,000 in capital and used 75 tons of steel and 14 railroad cars of cement. When all that was over, the 7,500-seat Greenlee Field stood on Bedford Avenue in the Hill.

It was a baseball palace, particularly compared to what most Negro League teams were accustomed to.

The Hill is only a 5 or 10-minute walk from downtown, an even shorter commute by streetcar, by far the best location available to Rooney's pro football team in 1932. And so, Rooney turned to Greenlee, another sporting man about town, setting up a sublime instance of table turning: a white owner renting a ballpark from a black one.

The men maintained a life-long friendship. When Greenlee died in 1952, Rooney was a pallbearer at his funeral.

§

Rooney's team was not the only sandlot team in Pittsburgh—there were semi-pro community sandlot teams all over Western Pennsylvania, some of which were black and provided the only outlet for black players from 1934 to 1946. The Steelers joined the NFL in 1933. The next year, team owners agreed to segregate what had previously been an integrated operation at the behest of known bully and racist, George Preston Marshall (owner of the then Boston Redskins, now the Washington franchise). There weren't many black players on NFL rosters, but there were a few sprinkled throughout the teams (though not on Marshall's team).

None of those men were invited to play the 1934 season, including Pittsburgh's Ray Kemp.

After WWII, in 1946, teams started signing black players in dribs and drabs. By 1962, the league was fully reintegrated, at which time owners denied that there had ever been any hiring ban whatsoever. Even the beloved Art Rooney denied it, saying that black players were too hard to find, all evidence to the contrary.

As a result of the little discussed, shameful era of segregation in the NFL, community teams like the Delaney Rifles, East Liberty Scholastics, and East End Athletics sprang up all over Pittsburgh providing opportunity for African American footballers. The most enduring of Pittsburgh's sandlot teams was the Garfield Eagles who were, according to historian local Rob Ruck, the finest black football team in Western Pennsylvania from 1928 to the mid-1940s. Some players were so good, in fact, that they were occasional hired guns for white community teams like the Carrick Eagles and the Tarentum Firemen.

These local, semi-pro teams had deep roots where they played. The stage was smaller. The players often lived and worked there, too. They were invested in their neighborhoods and the neighborhoods were invested in them. This is especially true of black teams, given the segregation of the sport and further racial divides along neighborhood lines. There are countless stories of shop owners and entrepreneurs giving or lending money to a player who was between jobs or behind on his rent; there were neighborhood dances and dinners to support the team. It was all for one and one for all. The Eagles were Garfield. And Garfield was them.

The Eagles, like the Crawfords and Grays and Steelers, shaped and built this layered story of sport, integral to the story of Pittsburgh. They are essential to Pittsburgh's love affair with football, a love that took hold deeply and organically, street by street, block by block, neighborhood by neighborhood and sandlot by sandlot.

§

Women's football is new, but it is not so new as I originally thought when I started writing about the Passion. In 1968, women's basketball was still a bizarre, bastardized version of the game that more resembled foursquare than the men's game. Mia Hamm wasn't even born. Five more years would pass before the watershed 'Battle of the Sexes' tennis match between Billie Jean King and Bobby Riggs. *Ms. Magazine* had yet to be founded.

Yet in 1968, a full four years prior to the signing of Title IX, women suited up and played full-contact football in Pittsburgh.

Twenty years after the fact, in a 1989 story in the *Pittsburgh Post-Gazette*, one former Pittsburgh Powderkeg player described what drove her: "I loved the game.... the harder you hit, the less you get hurt. It was exhausting at first, but you love it so much you go, go, go." Another said, "The first time I got knocked to the ground, I felt like I had been hit by a car. When I got up and found I wasn't broken, I thought I was a superwoman or something."

The Powderkegs were a full-contact football team, using the same rulebook as men. The players were paid $15 or $30 per game and played against the Detroit Fillies, the Toronto Canadian Belles, the Midwest Cowgirls and a few others. They were coached by former Steelers fullback Charley Scales whose staff included whoever he was able to hector into lending a hand that day.

Like the Passion, the Powderkegs practiced three nights a week, usually at Brookline's Moore Field, but they played their games at South Stadium, now known as Cupples, home of the Passion. Back then the field was in much worse shape. "Dirt. It was dirt," laughed former Powderkeg Rae Hodge when we sat down to talk. "It was rough, it was a rugged thing." All these years in between and Hodge still lit up talking about her football days. "You have to protect your teammates. You have to be in a certain place. If you don't, it impacts someone else's health. What other game does that? What other game puts you in a position like you are when you're on the football field?"

Now a Presbyterian minister, Hodge joined the team in 1970 when one of her co-workers at Westinghouse convinced her to try it out. Thus she embarked on a great, unexpected adventure, a time when she was a tight end, a kicker, a punter, and the backup QB. Whatever the team needed, she would do. It was a time she describes as wicked, amazing and the most wonderful time, maybe even the best of times. One thing is certain: Hodge and her teammates were women ahead of their time—way, way ahead of their time.

Through their four seasons (1968 through 1971) they won as many games as they lost, led by QB Ronnie Garner, described in the *Washington* (Pennsylvania) *Observer-Reporter* as, "Pittsburgh's stylish QB." Hodge remembers her simply as their awesome QB. "She was a powerful woman. She could throw the ball 50 yards."

At a time when virtually no men's teams started an African American at quarterback, Pittsburgh's Ronnie Garner was a black woman.

Beyond the fact that they were women playing football, the team was racially mixed and their togetherness on the football field spilled over into real life. They all hung out, this group of women, sometimes at some sketchy joints, often at the long-gone Silver Buckle bar in Uptown. This was the late 1960s and 1970s, a time when racial tensions were boiling over in cities all across America. Yet, there they were, black women and white women, cops and dancers, playing football and developing friendships.

Certainly, some looked askance at the Powderkegs, even though not one of the women did it out of a political agenda; they were chasing something harder to pin down, that sense of feeling like 'a superwoman.' For all the macho posturing, chest-thumping, and stereotypical dumb-jock mentality that has come to be associated with the sport, there is also the power of the collective and the freedom found in great physical effort. Sublimating one's ego in pursuit of team goals gave each of them a pure, inexplicable joy.

"I felt invincible. It was a wonderful feeling—to go all out, throwing yourself around," said Hodge.

But there just wasn't enough support at the dawning of the 1970s, and there wasn't enough money to be made. When the team folded in 1971, all the Powderkegs felt a profound sense of loss. "It took a long time to get over," Hodge recalled. "I was at loose ends. It was grieving, that's exactly what it was—grieving. I didn't realize that's what it was. It was not being with everyone and not playing the game, just not playing the game. That was a tough time, a really tough time."

Though nearly 40 years have passed since Rae Hodge and Ronnie Garner set foot on the gridiron at South, the Passion still battle some of the same stereotypes and misconceptions about what women can do and, even, what is appropriate for them to aspire to do, but back when the Powderkegs played, the questions and comments were more pointed: Why would a woman want to do that? Or perhaps, *what kind of woman* wants to do that? To me, it just was what it appeared to be—a group of Pittsburgh women, both black and white, wanting to test themselves by doing something completely new, running wild, throwing themselves around with abandon, being completely and totally free.

§

Nobody's ever been able to fully answer the why of it—why play? why Pittsburgh?—but the Pittsburgh Passion owner, T. Conn helped me to see the how of it and specifically, how it works in Pittsburgh. Conn herself had an 'aha' moment when she was inducted into the Western Pennsylvania Semi-Pro Football Hall of Fame (just the second woman, after Rae Hodge). That day, she started seeing her own team along this historical continuum, the Powderkegs and the Hope-Harveys, the Crawfords and the Garfield Eagles. "There are lots of people ahead of us who paved the way," she said. "I didn't realize how far back it went. Some of these guys played football for a gazillion years. I know now everybody looks at the Steelers, but they went through a history—they worked all day and played football at night. Most of the guys who were there were like 80-plus, but they played football back then with no paychecks. I think they related to us. It's kind of nice to see these old men and you would think they would be like, 'girls don't play football.' Instead they were standing up and saying, 'let's give it up for the Passion.' That's crossing some barriers."

That, and connecting some dots through Pittsburgh's history. to be presented in a way that's news. We're not Sinclair Lewis's Midwest. We're not the chamber of commerce Midwest anymore either, despite what the chamber of commerce would have you believe. We're the Rust Belt, and bad stuff has happened to us, we have stories to tell, and we're not dead yet.

So much of Southern literature come from that impulse: "You conquered us, but fuck you." It's more, "Fuck New York, let's read about ourselves, let's support our people, let's make it a real priority to read the books." The Midwest still doesn't have that kind of swagger, but it's the kind of thing that can be championed in a non-boosterish way.

Banjos on the North Side

Nico Chiodi

They say that Pittsburgh is the City of Bridges, with 446 bridges spanning the three rivers and many creeks leading to them. There is the Hot Metal Bridge, leading from downtown to South Side; the Fort Pitt Bridge passing directly by the blockhouse built in the 1760s. There's also Washington's Crossing, a bridge close to where George Washington crossed the Allegheny River in 1753; and finally there are the Liberty and Veterans bridges. But there is one that is not so apparent as the Three Sisters bridges, which span the Allegheny and make a striking postcard. It is our metaphorical bridge to the past. We live in a town of the new, of the up and coming, of the high-tech; but none of us have forgotten our past, or what this town once was. Pittsburgh is unique in that aspect and not for the reasons most people would think.

A quarter of a century ago, a man who was born in Pittsburgh returned after a long career in New York. He found, to his disappointment, that there was no place for him to play his four-string banjo with other musicians. Being the performer that he was, he started a club for local four-string banjo players to meet and play together. He placed an ad in the paper—six men answered the call—and the Pittsburgh Banjo Club was formed.

Several years passed, and word got around. They discovered there were lots of other lonely banjo players around Pittsburgh, people who had learned while playing at the weekly rehearsals, or those who had played the banjo already. The Club started doing shows at community events, as well as at nursing and retirement homes, where their obvious audiences remembered this music when it was sung by their parents. They kept any money they made after donations were made to charity. As great as that fact is, there are over 80 banjo clubs across the country, and many of them donate. However, none have achieved the popularity and beloved status that the Pittsburgh Banjo Club has.

In the North Side Elks Lodge, where the Banjo Club has its rehearsals (open to the public every Wednesday at 8 p.m.), there is a bar and a community room. The audience sits at tables in the community room, clapping, singing, talking and laughing for the two and a half hour rehearsal. These tables are all like mini bridges to the past. At first, mostly those of the older generation filled the chairs. These were the people who had very precious memories associated with the music because their parents and grandparents had grown up listening to and playing it. But word got around, and soon the younger, college-aged crowd started showing up. They surprisingly found that though it wasn't the folksy bluegrass/country banjo that has made a resurgence in popular culture that they were accustomed to hearing, they greatly enjoyed it.

Because the older crowd was scattered throughout the room, many of the young people had nowhere else to sit but next to or across from them, therefore the bridges were built. The music, closeness and, yes, perhaps the libations, create an atmosphere where it is almost impossible not to engage with your fellow audience members. Instead of focusing on their differences, the generations began to realize what made them alike. It was as if each tiny table that made up the long ones was a bridge itself, bringing the old to the young and the past to the present, thus making up the giant bridge that is the Pittsburgh Banjo Club.

"Other than [the music], I enjoy the people," Heather Walsh, a relative newcomer to the Banjo Club, says. "You find college students and folks in their nineties, skinny jean wearing hipsters, tattooed and pierced musicians, business people, "Grandpa Joe" and the mayor... and everyone is mingling and getting along."

JoAnn Azinger, Treasurer of the Club, and wife of one of the founding members (though she herself does not play) also handles the 50/50 drawing each week, and therefore talks to many of the both new and old audience members, agrees. "There isn't a stigma, like, if somebody comes in... all tattooed up, or they've got earrings in their nose...

it doesn't seem like [people say] 'ooh, don't sit near me,' it's all part of the familiarity. When people walk through that door, it's like a whole different world."

Norm Azinger, founding member, musical director, and husband of JoAnn Azinger, says he enjoys the Club. "It's a chance to play [the banjo] and the camaraderie with the other people. The people were always fun. We always have a good time.... It's a fun time, always a fun time."

So if you come to Pittsburgh to our LEED-certified convention center to discuss medical advances from University of Pittsburgh Medical Center; robotics with Carnegie Mellon Univeristy engineers; or to learn how to remake a city with the Green Building Alliance, then take a ride across a bridge to the North Side. Come see the bridge to the past that has made it to several top ten lists of reasons to visit or live in Pittsburgh. Visit the Pittsburgh Banjo Club and be transported back to the 1920s. Come meet Frank Rossi, the founder and charismatic leader. Say hello to the 15-year-old boy, who was playing banjo on stage since he was eight years old, who is lucky enough to be a part of it: my name is Nico and I'll be sitting in the second row.

Is Pittsburgh America's Most Livable City?

Sean Posey

American *news coverage* of the meteoric rise of Chinese industry might invariably focuses on the soot and smog-ridden manufacturing cities of the Middle Kingdom. Photographs of cities like Shenzhen and Harbin flash across television screens, looking like stills from some level of Dante's *Inferno*. While this might promote some smugness among Americans, it was only a few generations ago that American manufacturing cities resembled hellish nightmares, where the environment and the working class were abused in equal measure. Most notable among those was Pittsburgh, America's "steel city."

In a little over a hundred years, Pittsburgh went from "hell with the lid off," to a symbol of America's collapsing steel sector in the 1980s. However, today the Burgh has been rebranded "America's most livable city." But is it? What's behind this Rust Belt success story?

The days where Pittsburgh was shrouded in haze and surrounded by towering steel mills is long over. Today, "eds and meds," a robust non-profit sector, biotech and robotics are part of a diversified economy that is light years away from the economic monoculture of a few decades ago. Especially within the last ten years, Pittsburgh has weathered the recent economic downturn far better than most cities. It has also successfully rebranded itself, with a large dose of help from the media.

Pittsburgh has recently been branded the "miracle city," "America's smartest city," and "America's most livable city," the latter by *Forbes* and *The Economist*. [1] The accolades have come in droves, but the city's renaissance is decades in the making and highly uneven.

Already by 1940, population growth had flatlined in the city. Pittsburgh's job growth also trailed other major metropolitan areas of the era. [2] In response, the city fathers began to plan for a post-war physical renewal of the city, as well as a transition to a much more diversified economy. This included urban renewal projects for the downtown area; the first real efforts at environmental remediation, and the creation of new skyscrapers and underground parking garages. Known as "Renaissance," this was the first of two post-war renewal plans. In the 1970s, a second more informal plan known as Renaissance II was under way. One of the most important outcomes of Renaissance II was the creation of a civic coalition that helped galvanize the initial plans for a Pittsburgh beyond steel, something that never happened during Renaissance I. According to social historian Roy Lubove, "Renaissance II was an extraordinary episode in American urban history. It marked a widespread commitment on the part of a city's public and private leaders to abandon its industrial past and create a new economy and cultural identity." [3]

Despite a forward thinking civic and business coalition, the demise of the local steel industry in the 1980s utterly devastated the city. By 2000, the city had lost 80 percent of its peak steel workforce. [4] The collapse of the steel industry essentially drove an entire generation from the city. By the '80s, over 90 percent of the city's neighborhoods had lost population. [5] The city went from a peak population of 676,806 in 1950 to 305,704 in 2010. Yet, after over three decades of investment and restructuring, Pittsburgh's fortunes began to change in the new century.

Compared to its Rust Belt compatriots, the city does look good. Pittsburgh's downtown weathered deindustrialization far better than almost any other similar city, and it retains a large daytime workforce. Some of the most prestigious Fortune 500 companies are headquartered in the city. Aside from Pittsburgh's well-known "eds and meds sector," there is also a robust energy sector, a steel technology cluster, and a vibrant biotechnology industry, which are all part of the city's new economy.

Pittsburgh also retains its enormous cultural offerings, including theater, dance and ballet, as well as first-rate museums like the Carnegie Museum of Art, the Andy Warhol Museum, and the Carnegie Museum of Natural History—one of the top-ranked natural history museums in the nation. The city also boasts an impressive number of historic landmarks, including the Phipps Conservatory and Botanical Garden, which includes the world's only Platinum-certified LEED greenhouse.

Despite its enormous population loss, Pittsburgh's neighborhoods, on the whole, are stronger and more intact than those of cities that have suffered similar population declines (Detroit, St. Louis, Cleveland, and Youngstown). The city's incredible gains in education are undeniable. In 1970, Pittsburgh ranked fifty-fifth in high school graduation rates out of 120 metro areas, but in 2006 they were number three. In 1970, Pittsburgh ranked sixty-ninth among metro areas in percentages of people with college degrees, by 2006, it was number thirty-six. [6] In 2009, the city was chosen as the host site for the G-20 summit. Pittsburgh had truly arrived.

The question of whether or not Pittsburgh is the most "livable" city is hard to answer. *Forbes* loves its "most" lists, especially when they convey something negative. Cities either tout their high rankings or question the entire system when they rank lowly on the lists. However, examining Pittsburgh's merits is certainly fair game. "Livable for whom?" might be the better question.

Pittsburgh's still has notable problems. For over a decade, it has been an Act 47 city—classified as a financially distressed municipality. Despite immense progress, the city still has a large pension shortfall. Considering Pittsburgh's size, it has an extremely small foreign-born population—below six percent—typical for a Rust Belt city. From the 2012 Census estimates it appears the city finally has stopped shrinking, though it gained only about 150 people between 2010 and 2012. As the *Pittsburgh Post-Gazette* put it, "If the city of Pittsburgh is no longer the anchor dragging down the county's and region's population, it's hardly the engine driving a resurgence, either." [7]

Pittsburgh's "invisible communities," are suffering from a variety of socioeconomic problems that essentially are part of an entirely different city than the one described by *Forbes* or *The Economist*. While Pittsburgh might be the "next big food town," according to *Bon Appétit*, it is already a city with enormous problems for low-income communities trying to access healthy food. [8] The city leads the nation in percentage of residents living in neighborhoods with "low supermarket access." [9] The problem extends to the region as a whole. Pittsburgh's Just Harvest, an anti-hunger advocacy and organizing group, refers to statistics that "depict a region in which access to healthy food appears to be more of a privilege than a right of all citizens." [10]

Pittsburgh's invisible communities are also disproportionately affected by crime. As a whole, the city has lower violent crime rates than most Rust Belt cities of its size. Violent crime is concentrated in more distressed neighborhoods like Homewood, the Hill District, and in neighborhoods on the North Side. Pittsburgh's overall murder rate is around five per 100,000, but the murder rate for black men is 284 per 100,000—that's 50 times the national average. [11]

While Pittsburgh diverges from Cleveland in many ways, its dismal African American infant mortality rate mirrors its neighbor to the north. In the US, black children are twice as likely to die in infancy than white children. In Pittsburgh, that number is five times greater. For Allegheny County, the infant mortality rate for black people is worse than infant mortality rates in Mexico or China. [12] And this is happening in a city with a notable healthcare sector and some of the best hospitals in the region—University of Pittsburgh Medical Center is the number one ranked hospital in the state.

The aforementioned problems are of course connected to Pittsburgh's extreme poverty problem. While *The Economist* and *Forbes* rolled out their most livable columns, the U.S. Census Bureau announced that Pittsburgh led the nation in poverty rates among African Americans ages 18-64. It also has the highest percentage of black children under the age of five living in poverty. [13]

Pittsburgh's recent history is a mix of remarkable success and remarkable failure. The city's title of "America's most livable city" seems to be a story of haves and have-nots. Pittsburgh's initial experience with industrialization is comparable to many other Rust Belt cities, but the city's political, business, and nonprofit communities managed to make organized and thoughtful plans for a post-industrial Pittsburgh. There is quite a lesson for other cities to learn from this. However, it took Pittsburgh decades to bring the city to the position it is today, and clearly it has a long way to go. The city's different demographics also make it hard to compare to places like Detroit, Cleveland, or St. Louis. The "Burgh," both hobbled and hopeful, has moved to the head of the pack of America's former industrial giants—but not everyone is coming along for the ride.

References

[1] "Pittsburgh Ranked Smartest City in America," *Pittsburgh Magazine*, June 25, 2013 http://www.pittsburghmagazine.com/Best-of-the-Burgh-Blogs/The-412/June-2013/Pittsburgh-Ranked-Smartest-City-in-America/ (Accessed January 25, 2014).

[2] E.M. Hoover, *Economic Study of the Pittsburgh Region. Vol. 1*, Region in Transition. (Pittsburgh: University of Pittsburgh Press, 1963).

[3] Roy Lubove, *Twentieth Century Pittsburgh, Volume Two: The Post-Steel Era* (Pittsburgh: University of Pittsburgh Press, 1996), IX.

[4] David J. Lynch, "Pittsburgh's Heart of Steel Still Beats Among Transformed City," *USA Today*, September 29, 2009. http://usatoday30.usatoday.com/money/economy/2009-09-21-us-steel-pittsburgh_N.htm (Accessed January 26, 2014).

[5] Sabina Deitrick, "Case Study: Pittsburgh Goes High Tech," in *Rebuilding America's Legacy Cities: New Directions for the Industrial Heartland*, ed. Allan Mallach (New York, NY: The American Assembly, 2012), 82.

[6] Federal Reserve Bank of Chicago. "Growth and Great Lakes Cities,"http://midwest.chicagofedblogs.org/archives/2009/01/great_lakes_met.html (Accessed January 27, 2014).

[7] Gary Rotstein, "Pittsburgh's Population Moves Upward-by 152," *Pittsburgh Post Gazette*, May 23, 2013. http://www.post-gazette.com/hp_mobile/2013/05/23/Pittsburgh-population-moves-upward-by-152/stories/201305230230 (Accessed January 26, 2014).

[8] Andrew Knowlton, The Foodist, "The Foodist Predicts the Next Big Ingredients in 2014," *bon appétit*, December 18, 2013. http://www.bonappetit.com/columns/the-foodist/slideshow/foodist-trendy-ingredient-predictions-2014/?slide=4 (Accessed January 28, 2014).

[9] U.S. Department of the Treasury, CDFI Fund, *Searching for Markets: The Geography of Inequitable Access to Healthy and Affordable Food in the United States.* 2012. http://www.cdfifund.gov/what_we_do/resources/SearchingForMarkets_Report_web_Low_%20Res.pdf (Accessed January 29, 2014).

[10] Zachary Murray, *A Menu for Food Justice: Strategies for Improving Access to Healthy Foods in Allegheny* Pittsburgh, PA: Just Harvest, 2013).

[11] Allegheny County Department of Human Services, *Violence in Allegheny County and Pittsburgh*. (Pittsburgh, 2008).

[12] Timothy Williams, "Tackling Infant Mortality Rates Among Blacks," *New York Times*, October 14, 2011. http://www.nytimes.com/2011/10/15/us/efforts-to-combat-high-infant-mortality-rate-among-blacks.html?pagewanted=all&_r=0 (Accessed January 30, 2014).

[13] Harold D. Miller, "Regional Insights: High Black Poverty a Shame," *Pittsburgh Post Gazette*, July 4, 2010. http://www.post-gazette.com/Biz-opinion/2010/07/04/Regional-Insights-High-black-poverty-a-shame/stories/201007040132 (Accessed January 29, 2014).

Steel City Fandom

Brendan Hykes
Illustrated by Chris Brown

It's early on a Saturday afternoon in the warehouse-sized exhibition hall of a convention center. The air smells of stationery and sweat. Tables are set up in long rows, and the crowd files along them, looking down at whatever is laid out in front of them. One or two people sit behind each table watching, smiling and greeting anyone who meets their gaze. Sometimes someone will stop to browse or chat and the whole line has to shift around them.

A young woman gives a friendly smile from her seat. Set up in front of her is an array of booklets, printed out in black-and-white, on a fairly good quality paper, and stapled together. She's making casual conversation with a man who lazily flips through a booklet.

"So are you from around here?" she asks, before catching herself. "Oh, I almost missed the Steelers shirt."

He smiles with Pittsburgh pride and then asks what her comic books are about.

At the table next to her, an obviously married couple, probably in their late thirties, are selling everything from bowties to coasters, refrigerator magnets to small purses, all made from the pages of old comic books.

A few aisles down are the many booths stocked with long boxes full of comics. Collectors are hunched over, flipping through back issues of Punisher, Spawn, Green Arrow and so on, looking for that one gem

they've been missing.

Just down from the comics are tables covered in action figures: He-Man, Teenage Mutant Ninja Turtles and WWF. Nerf guns, plastic lightsabers and tricorders. A twenty-something grabs a Venkman figure excitedly, squeezing one arm making the Ghostbuster character's plastic jaw drop and the hair stick up from its head.

The only empty space is taken up by a group of at least a dozen teenagers who have sat down on the floor. Some of them are hunched over their phones, off in their own digital worlds. One kid pokes the girl next to him and shows her a picture; she grins and nudges the kid next to her; the first kid leans over to show him the picture of a favorite character costume. They all giggle.

At the far end of the room against the wall are the celebrities. There's the guy who played Featured Zombie #5 in one of the better-known zombie movies, one of the original Power Rangers and at least two pro wrestlers. People are lined up to talk to all of them.

Out of the corner of your eye is Steel Man (or is it Burgh Man? Some Pittsburgh superhero...) in full black and gold costume, regaling some kids.

This is a convention but Comic Con is what most people would call it. Maybe you're at Steel City Con, where there are a lot more celebrities and a lot more toys. Or maybe you're at Pittsburgh Comic Con, in which case there are more comics than toys and a few less celebrities (but not by much).

If the comics being sold feature talking animals, and there's more than a few people walking around in animal costumes, you're probably at Anthrocon, the world's largest furry convention. If the signs are all in Japanese, and the costumes are all anime characters, you might be at Tekko, the anime convention.

If everyone's dressed up like zombies, it's probably Zombie Fest. Shrink the size of the room, remove all of the celebrities, costumers, toys and vendors, then add a few more indie cartoonists, and you're at PIX, the Pittsburgh Indy Comics Expo. Replace all the comics with Sci-Fi and fantasy novels and the cartoonists with authors, and you're likely at Confluence, Pittsburgh's literary Sci-Fi and fantasy convention.

Comic conventions have been around for a while. The first were held in the '60s and '70s. These were small events run by fans for fans. Sometimes it was just an opportunity for people to get together, meet like-minded fans and talk about the comics they loved. Often it was an opportunity to meet the writers and artists responsible for those comics. Over the decades, they got bigger and more popular.

Pittsburgh's own comic convention was founded in 1994 and held at the Radisson and ExpoMart in Monroeville. Later it moved to the Monroeville Convention Center. By then, several other conventions such as Confluence and the Pittsburgh Toy, Comic and Childhood Collectibles Show (which would later be renamed the Steel City Con) had been around for several years.

As conventions became more popular and more common, they also began to cater to more specific fandoms. First held in 2003, Tekkoshocon (later renamed Tekko) focuses primarily on anime and manga, Japanese comics and animation, as well as Otaku, or Japanese-influenced culture.

2006 saw the first world record zombie walk, which would eventually evolve into Zombie Fest, a convention revolving around the living dead. That was also the first year Anthrocon was held in Pittsburgh. The first PIX, focusing solely on independently produced comics, was held in 2010.

In the '90s and early aughts, Pittsburgh Comic-Con brought in some of the biggest names in comics. They even hosted the Harvey Awards (one of the two biggest awards in comics, named for cartoonist Harvey Kurtzman) from 2000 to 2002. However, due to funding shortages, the awards ceremony was cancelled in 2003. They moved the MoCCA fest to New York the following year.

The convention suffered an even greater blow in 2007, when co-promoter Michael George was arrested for murder (and eventually

sentenced to life in prison). His wife continued to run the convention in later years. While attendance would eventually return to the numbers they had with the Harvey Awards, they weren't able to keep up with in ever-growing attendance that seemed to be happening elsewhere.

At the same time, Steel City Con was branching out from toys and collectibles to comics and pop culture. Initially a trade show, they now pack in a large lineup of celebrities. The main exhibit area is still filled with mostly vendors, but there are more artists and comics, and the aisles are lined with fans and cosplayers.

Cosplay is when fans dress up as their favorite characters, making their own variations. Sometimes they'll dress as gender-swapped versions (female Doctor Who or male Emma Frost). Sometimes they'll merge two characters or concepts (Sailor Moon meets Captain America, or zombie Disney princesses).

Cosplay got popular in the US in the '90s, mostly in the anime community, before branching out into the comics and video game community. Now it's become an industry in its own right. At Steel City Con, you might see a family in Penguins gear lining up to get their picture taken with a group of Stormtroopers, chatting with them about whether the team has a chance of making the playoffs this year. Pittsburgh even has its own branch of Ghostbusters.

Tekko holds a convention-long LARP (live-action role-playing game), where attendees who sign up ahead of time can play as an anime character of their choosing. While neither Confluence nor PIX sees much in the way of cosplay during the convention, Confluence does host an annual costume contest. Most people assume Anthrocon would be the most costume-oriented convention, but furry fandom isn't nearly as focused on costume as you'd think. Organizer Samuel Conway estimates that only about 20 percent of attendees come in garb.

Anthrocon was first held in Albany, New York in 1997, and moved around a lot due to its rapid growth in attendance (their first year saw somewhere around 300 attendees and by their fourth they were over 1,000. In 2014 they saw nearly 6,000). Conway says that Pittsburgh lobbied hard to win over the convention, and since moving to the David L. Lawrence Convention Center in 2006, they found the city so welcoming that they've gone so far as to adopt the city's colors of black and gold for their corporate flag.

Now, on one weird weekend in July, it's not uncommon to walk into a downtown Primanti's and see a table full of fur suits, hollow animal heads and paws stacked on the floor.

In the early aughts, conventions were quickly growing from simple fan gatherings to bigger and bigger media events. Movies started getting involved. Video games. Actors would show up to sign autographs and meet fans. For slick organizers, conventions were becoming big money.

Anthrocon is a non profit and Tekko is run by the Pittsburgh Japanese Culture Society, also a non profit. PIX doesn't charge for admission or exhibitor tables. The expo is run by the Toonseum, a museum in downtown Pittsburgh dedicated to cartoon art.

While Pittsburgh Comic Con raised money for charity every year, it was announced in 2015 that they had been purchased by Wizard Entertainment, a national publicly-traded corporation, and would become one of their Wizard World conventions. Ironically, in 2001 Frank Miller concluded his keynote Harvey Awards speech by tearing up a copy of *Wizard Magazine*, published by the same Wizard Entertainment.

The transition to Wizard World has some local creators concerned. Wizard World doesn't always have the best reputation. The table costs are higher and they try to bring in a lot more celebrities. However, others welcome the change. Many creators had refused to attend the convention previously due to Michael George's involvement, and others felt that the convention had grown stale over the years. State College, PA-based artist Jason Lenox has attended Wizard World in Philadelphia a few times, and thinks this change will be for the better.

Each convention has its own lineup of panels, events and exhi-

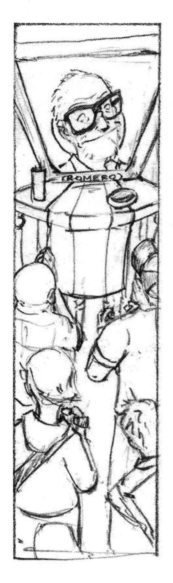

bitions. Anthrocon has a parade, dance and programming that includes workshops on art and writing, animation, puppeteering and costume design. There is also panel discussion on many topics, which are often suggested by members. In the past, Pittsburgh Comic Con has hosted a costume contest, poker tournaments, artist quick-sketch events and Q&A sessions with creators.

PIX is only held for a day, and the exhibitor tables close up in the late afternoon to make room for the panel discussions in the evening. Confluence holds panels on any number of subjects related to fantasy and science-fiction, as well as filk (folk music focusing on sci-fi and fantasy) concerts. In 2015, they will be hosting the Super Smash Opera, a musical based on the Nintendo fighting game.

Tekko holds an AMV (anime music video) contest, a dance competition and cosplay contest. They also hold concerts with Japanese bands and musicians known for creating theme songs for anime series. Zombie Fest holds a zombie walk, zombie dance party and hosts local bands.

The atmosphere at each convention is different. Steel City is a warehouse-sized venue filled with vendors selling toys and games and comics and collectibles. A smaller room holds "Artist's Alley" and the celebrity guests. Attendees line up for meet-and-greet and photo ops with TV stars, horror movie monsters and sci-fi cinema icons.

Pittsburgh has been a similar style convention, with much less focus on commerce and much greater focus on comics. There are a lot more writers and artists. Fans will come to meet a favorite creator, but they'll also come to browse through the aisles of self-published creators, artists offering prints and on-site commissions and smaller publishers.

Anthrocon also has a dealer area where fans can find artists, toy vendors, and costume supply and accessory vendors. They have a large area, referred to as "the Zoo," meant for socializing. Per Samuel Conway, "Anthrocon (and furry fandom in general) is extremely community-oriented." The atmosphere is a family friendly one. "It is important to us that anyone who attends the convention feels comfortable and safe."

Zombie Fest, on the other hand, makes it clear that they are a PG-13 event. The costumes are graphic, the bands that play are loud, and the event serves beer.

Zombie Fest is run by the *It's Alive* show, a late night chiller theater type show. Initially holding a Zombie walk at the Monroeville Mall, where the zombie classic *Dawn of the Dead* was filmed, it has since expanded into a two-day event held in downtown Pittsburgh. They held the Guinness World Record (and lost it, and regained it, and so on) for largest zombie walk and largest gathering of zombies.

PIX is a much smaller event, held for one day in a single venue in Pittsburgh's South Side. There aren't any cosplayers, vendors or toys. Everyone who has a table is a creator, writer, artist, or all of the above. Many of the art and comics being sold are of a more personal nature.

There are less superhero and horror books; instead you'll find a comic that tells the story of a relationship through the meals a couple shared together, or exploration of maturity via a black hole appearing on someone's living room wall. This is the indie music of comic books. They're very pure to comics, and heavily identified with the Pittsburgh arts and comics scene.

Of course, this being Pittsburgh, wherever you go you'll find black and gold. Whether it's the black and yellow of Anthrocon's flag, or a superhero logo redone in Pittsburgh colors. And let's not forget Steel Man and Burgh Man, Pittsburgh's own superheroes. Burgh man wears a black and gold superhero costume, and Steel Man's costume is based on the uniforms worn in the steel mills. Both can be seen at local conventions; meeting with fans, making balloon animals or passing out comics to kids.

The biggest attraction of these fan events might be the chance to hang out with people who are into the same things as you. Or it might be the chance to run into any number of surprising celebrities. Once at Steel City Con, an artist told a story of how Tom Savini (a legendary, local makeup artist best known for his horror film work) had stopped by her face-painting booth to compliment her work. Maybe you just want to dig up that classic back issue, or find a favorite toy from childhood, or get a print of a favorite character for your wall. Lots of people come out to support indie comics, meet the new artists and writers, or meet up with creators you only get a chance to see at conventions.

And, of course, there are plenty of Pittsburghers who will show up just because it's something to do on a Saturday afternoon.

Sitting in traffic on the way home you might notice Thor driving the car next to you. You might see kids in the backseat of the van in front of you playing with their new action figures, pretending to do battle with supervillains. And the guy that honks his horn and calls you a jagoff from his window is just as likely to be in a *Deadpool* T-shirt as a Steelers jersey.

These days just about every major city has at least one convention of their own. Pittsburgh has plenty, and while each one is unique, they're all uniquely Pittsburgh.

Chasing the Illusion

Cody McDevitt

Slots ring. The shouts of winners and losers fill the vast room. Some have lost their mortgage payment. A few leave with enough money for a trip to some exotic location bereft of the extreme jubilation and despair at this casino on Pittsburgh's North Shore.

Gordon Nored felt the despair. He had lost that night at craps. He stood back from the table, watching as other players continued to place their bets.

"Everyone is chasing an illusion," Nored said. "I believe the casinos in Pittsburgh, with most cities, the casinos pretty much suck our city dry. It's like that carrot on a stick…you have to let people get the carrot, to keep the illusion going. Most people who go to the casino wouldn't mind going on without it. It makes you wonder why you gamble to begin with when you just want your money back."

Casinos are big business in Western Pennsylvania. The two largest casinos in the Pittsburgh area—Rivers Casino on the North Shore and Meadows Racetrack and Casino in Washington County—have made close to $300 million from table games and slot machines between January and June of 2014, according to the Pennsylvania Gaming Control Board.

Supporters of casinos say that gamblers would squander their money on bad bets regardless of whether there was a casino in town. They argue the casino is just concentrating gambling in one place. Before the casinos, there were always seedy back-room poker games where thousands of dollars were on the line. And trips to out-of-state casinos were the norm.

But the loss of money among local gamblers was not as systematic as it is now. The people placing bets are not as street smart as the people able to find the back room game.

Gamblers and gambling experts believe that gambling addiction has gotten worse, despite the absence of any statistical evidence. The casino's presence is still a point of contention.

Gamblers are often unwilling to come forth to talk about their addiction. Like poverty, alcoholism or drug abuse, there is a stigma attached to being a compulsive gambler—they're seen as people lacking self-control.

Gamblers are often portrayed by casino supporters as regular people who just need to control spending habits better. Gambling addiction is often not acknowledged as a mental health problem.

Nored, who has had many run-ins with the law and a lengthy criminal record, also has a gambling addiction to add to his troubles.

Nored, 35, says he's been hurt by the presence of the casinos. Because of Nored's gambling addiction, his significant other left him and took his children away. Though he'd been a gambler before the casinos came, he said his addiction has only gotten worse since they've come to town.

Nored thinks the casinos prey on certain people—the elderly, mentally ill and desperately lonely.

"When you come in and hear the bells and whistles, it's psychological warfare. It's sort of like a war going on there. When you come in, you hear ringing," he said. "You gamble on your emotions. Emotional people are victims. Elderly people are victims. Mentally challenged, elderly and lonely people are victims. Those types of people are everyday gamblers. Most of those people have mental health issues."

In the 1999 National Gambling Impact Study Commission Report, gambling is listed as a pathological behavior. The report urged legislators and public officials to protect citizens vulnerable to the addiction.

When you walk in, you'll see countless knockout women sitting at the Levels Bar at the Rivers Casino, drinking cocktails as the men who still have money offer to buy their next round. The bartenders work the line, hustling, even though they have to share any tip they earn with their equally hardworking or alternatively lazy co-workers. The digital poker game at the bar waits for a drunkard to ash his cigarette and decide whether to hit or hold.

One leggy blond in a black miniskirt and a pink sleeveless shirt came into the casinos in July. She fed eight $20 bills from her boyfriend into the slot poker machine. She lost it all within four minutes.

Jim P., a member of Gamblers Anonymous in Pittsburgh, said the nature of gambling addiction has changed.

"Up to about 30 years (ago), it was betting on sports cars. In the old days, it was horse races, and dice and so on," he said. "Nowadays most people have machine problems...A lot of people don't bother with the old stuff. That takes you down quick. You lose money quick."

The staff likes to talk about the casino's biggest losers. One bartender at the Rivers Casino recalled a conversation with a cashier about a high-profile businessman who lost $30,000 in 30 minutes. These events are not uncommon at the casino.

"You hear about it. The cocktail servers see it," said Shannon Plue, a former Rivers Casino employee. "They'll come back and tell the bartender. And then it gets around. It would happen about once a month with those kind of numbers."

Nored said gambling has changed for him and his friends since the casinos came to town. Before, there was a limit to how much a person could win or lose in Pittsburgh.

"It's not like you and your buddy gambling after work," Nored said. "If you play cards or blackjack or shoot dice on the porch, in those neighborhood games, most people spend two dollars or $20. But people don't lose as much as they would lose on a casino. The reason why is because most people in those neighborhood games would have minimum money. When you're in a casino, you're chasing a mirage. They're putting $100,000 worth of chips in your face."

Once a person is inside, the casinos compensate loyal gamblers with access to exclusive clubs and the occasional free drink and gift, encouraging people to bet more frequently and place larger wagers. The gambler just has to show a rewards card.

"They count on the regulars," Plue said. "That's why they have the comps. If you come in with (the card), you'll get better perks than the newcomer. And the casino will make more money off of everything the regulars buy."

In December 2014, Rivers Casino spokeswoman Emily Watts told the *Pittsburgh Tribune-Review* that they wanted to renew their free-fare sponsorship of the Port Authority's free-ride zone from downtown to the North Shore. In 2012, Rivers Casino agreed to underwrite free rides, along with the Pittsburgh Steelers organization. Civic leaders applauded the move because of the ease of travel and savings it provided to local residents.

"We appreciate the Pittsburgh Steelers and the Rivers Casino stepping up," Allegheny County executive Rich Fitzgerald told the *Pittsburgh Post-Gazette* at the time. "(The free fare zone) provides easy access to Heinz Field and the Rivers Casino, but also extends our Downtown to the North Side where residents and visitors can get to locations including the Community College of Allegheny County and the Carnegie Science Center."

But the ease of travel was yet another incentive for gambling addicts to go to the casinos to gamble. Though the move seems charitable on its face, in reality it was a smart business move aimed at attracting customers.

At the casinos, lovers lean over shoulders, urging one more hit, one more gamble. Give it one more chance, they implore. The smell of freshly lit cigarettes fills the room as the swarms move toward the complimentary beverage stand.

Casinos are places of dreams and nightmares, efforts and shortcomings, dashed hopes and things beyond the imagination. It's the clearest picture of humanity at its most desperate and euphoric.

A wide range of people come in: the high-rolling businessman in the power suit at the roulette table; the drug dealer doubling down at the craps table with money he made slinging heroin; the working stiff blowing his biweekly paycheck at the poker or blackjack table. Even public officials are seen there.

Former Braddock manager Ella Jones was caught on casino surveillance withdrawing more than $40,000 she allegedly stole from taxpayers, according to an article from the *Pittsburgh Tribune-Review*.

As nights wear on, some leave in sorrow while others enter with hope. The elevators to and from the garage bid a happy farewell to the loser and an enticing welcome to the would-be winner.

Rumor has it that a player for the Pittsburgh Steelers chose to have himself banned from the Rivers Casino because of his gambling addiction, an anonymous gambler said. A person on the banned list can be thrown out and prosecuted for trespassing.

The Rivers Casino is the big venue in Western Pennsylvania. But the Meadows Racetrack and Casino, 25 miles south of Pittsburgh near Washington, Pa., is another option for locals. The Washington County casino has more than 3,000 slot machines, 67 table games and a poker room with 14 tables, according to the casino's website. There is also a racetrack, a bowling alley and dining options.

Ben Roethlisberger has been seen there, as have a number of other wealthy people losing enormous amounts of money. One bartender recalled a man losing $300,000 in three hours at the blackjack table. Another remembered a person losing $125,000.

The Meadows casino is filled with grandfathers in wheelchairs, grandmothers on walkers and disabled people on scooters—all shuttling to burn a few more dollars despite the inconvenient travel from the bathroom to the machines. The janitors occasionally get called to the floor when geriatric gamblers soil themselves on the casino rugs, an anonymous bartender said.

Tom Meinart, the publicist for Meadows Casino, declined to comment for this essay. The publicist for Rivers Casino said it supported the mission of the Office of Compulsive and Problem Gambling at the Pennsylvania Gaming Control Board, which is dedicated to aiding problematic gamblers by giving them information about telephone help lines and making them aware of the dangers of gambling.

City and state government officials have praised the introduction of slots and casinos because of the influx of tax revenue. When totals for each are combined, the Meadows and Rivers made about $250 million from the slots between January and June, according to the Gaming Control Board. The state of Pennsylvania makes close to $750,000 a day from its 55 percent slot tax at both casinos.

State Sen. Jim Ferlo called the casinos a mixed blessing. He knows the drawbacks. But he remains a staunch supporter of the casinos and was an important figure in getting the Rivers Casino to come to Pittsburgh.

"We were losing a billion dollars a year. Whether we started or not, revenue was leaving the state (for other casinos)," Ferlo said. "It made no sense to me why we should see the loss of that revenue."

Ferlo said more jobs, revenue, and tourism are a result of the casinos. Casino revenue has also helped to pay for new sports arenas and stadiums.

He's not alone in noticing the benefits of casinos. The National Gambling Impact Study Commission Report stated:

"Sleepy backwaters have become metropolises almost overnight; skyscrapers rise on the beaches at once-fading tourist areas; legions of employees testify to the hope and opportunities that the casinos have brought them and their families..."

The report cites economic benefits, too. Since 2005, the state has directed 34 percent of slot revenue toward property tax relief. The city of Pittsburgh gets $10 million a year simply for hosting the casino. Casinos statewide have created close to 17,000 jobs, which has generated an additional $1.3 billion in tax revenue.

Ferlo acknowledged that casinos often overwhelm the senses and make it more likely for a person to wager money. He said people who don't watch themselves could become psychologically addicted.

"This is a lot of personal responsibility," he said. "There will be adverse social impacts. But I think a lot of people who involve themselves in impulsive behavior are going to do it regardless."

There are pushes to reform the way casinos operate. One of the prominent reformers in the state is Bill Kearney. Kearney is a former gambling addict and reformer pushing for state legislation requiring casinos to send monthly statements to gamblers who lose or win more than $500. He thinks rewards cards have exacerbated gambling addiction and sees the statements as a form of consumer protection to deter gamblers from going back after big losses.

"Back (in the day), they didn't comp the slot players," Kearney said. "Back then, the money came off the tables. The cards get these people hooked on the points to get more perks. It's the most expensive and costly addiction. A drug addict or alcoholic cannot spend as much as a gambling addict in an hour. 95 percent of the statements will show people losing money."

Kearney is skeptical about regulatory agencies overseeing the gambling industry.

"The Gaming Control Board is all about protecting the casinos. They couldn't care less about the consumer," Kearney said. "When you legalize casinos, it's like having that carnival ripping your kids off every day. Don't you want loved ones knowing how much loved ones are losing a month? The lawmakers need the revenue. They don't (care)."

Richard McGarvey, spokesman for the Gaming Control Board, said any decisions about new rules would be made by the legislature.

"Obviously we're the regulators. What the legislature passes, we'll enforce," McGarvey said. "Until the legislature passes, we won't enforce it. It's up to them. We don't take a position on it."

For the gamblers, there may not be much change in the near future. The temptation will remain strong, and the money will continue to dwindle until gambling is no longer possible for the week or day. They'll have to wait for the next paycheck.

Nored has noticed he and other gamblers spend less money on other things—clothes, cars and meals—because they use it at the casino. It's had an effect on everything in the city, he said.

"Our bars get less business. The mom-and-pop restaurant loses money," Nored said. "When it comes to department stores, they're not buying anything because of the gambling. If they win, they may buy a car. But that's only the smart winner that does that."

Hour of Love

Jess Craig

There is a green wrought-iron fence. Almost picket-like but sharper. More stern. There is a flowerbed: tall, red flowers surrounded by green shrubbery and low-growing Aztec grass. The smell of fresh mulch masks the smell of the city: sewage and gasoline. It is Saturday, early morning. For a mid-September day it is already stiflingly hot, but a cool and frequent breeze blows wrapping three flags around their poles as metal lightly rattles against metal. A monotonous *ping, ping, ping.* The wind whips the flowers, scattering torn petals across a cement bridge encased by short cement walls. Guard rails, painted red, guide pedestrians to two sets of double glass doors. Above the doors in thick engraved letters, a black sign reads ALLEGHENY COUNTY JAIL.

From a distance the Allegheny County Jail is an apartment complex or an office building: four consecutive brick buildings book-ended by sleek black-paneled windows. To the spotlight-wielding trauma helicopters that fly above the jail on their way to the local hospital, to the pollen-roofed cars and double-long Port Authority buses passing by, the jail is just another set of skylights in the cityscape of Pittsburgh. Where one expects tall barbed wire fences, there is a thick wall of green scenery and the Monongahela River. Where one expects elevated guard booths, there sits a golden bridge of Pittsburgh and a skyscraping UPMC office building. Where one expects isolation, there are two main streets of Pittsburgh — First and Second Avenue—where traffic is just beginning

51

to pick up, where horns are beeped for the first time this morning.

A few cars weave out of line to park against the scuffed curbs of the jail's campus, joining bicyclists who skid to a stop and force front tires into bike racks. Visitors on foot arrive with a faint glimmer of sweat across their forehead. The Port Authority bus rolls to a screeching stop, opens its doors, and releases a wave of cold air followed by a line of people who stumble out of their seats and find uneasy footing.

By 8:30, there is a gathering of about 40 people all eagerly awaiting their one hour visitation time that begins at nine o'clock. But these people do not resemble what you imagine of people waiting to enter a jail to speak with *criminals*. This gathering appears to be of people waiting for Sunday mass to start or for the grocery store to open, or for the first pitch of the baseball game to be thrown. A disorganized array of people making casual conversation, calling out distant greetings, exchanging smiles and waves with those who just entered the confines of the jail's campus. An elderly woman seemingly enthralled in a conversation shakes her cane by her side, a toddler risen from his bed too early leans against his mother's hip and pops handfuls of dry cereal into his mouth.

"Ready for them Bengals?" one man bellows, his arm swinging up by his face, his hand shaking as if he was cheering. The black and gold hat atop his head and the massive tattoo of the Steelers emblem on his right calf indicate he is an avid fan of his hometown's football team.

"C'mon Steelers," another man shouts out from a few feet away.

From behind a clustered group of lab coats, a father and son break off from the flow of pedestrian traffic. They slow in front of the jail and are immediately absorbed into the group. The father, an average middle-aged man with dark brown hair, wraps his arm around his son. No older than ten years, the little boy is dressed in a red *Iron Man* T-shirt, khaki shorts, and gray sneakers. He keeps up with his father's stride, and as the two move closer to the jail. A few women bend over to the little boy. "Hello, little guy," some shriek patting him on the shoulder or rustling his long blonde hair. "Cool shirt," others say.

The two find a spot just past the line of flag poles. They carry on a quiet conversation although they are frequently interrupted by men, women, and grandmothers coming up and shaking the father's hand or cracking a joke and then fleeing in laughter.

"How is everything?" one man asks the father, patting his shoulder while he asks.

The father sighs and looks down at his son. "Okay," he replies. "It's been tough for him," he says and nods his head. "People always askin' about his mom. Is your mom comin' to the soccer tournament, is your mom coming to teacher conference night?" The father pauses and watches his son stare up at a tiny window where his mother is looking down on him. "Other kids tease him, ask is your mom really in jail?"

"Yeah, kids'll be kids, you know?" the man replies and the two of them stand in silence, neither one wanting to admit that nobody ever outgrows those feelings.

"You see her room?" the father asks the son.

"I think so," the son replies. His voice is hoarse and he covers his mouth to cough into his hand. "Six, eleven," he repeats to his father pointing up towards the window he's been staring at since he arrived.

The boy is calm and complacent at the jail. He moves through the crowd following his father, smiling at others' concerns and averting his eyes when the grown-ups start talking serious. He is filled with a giddy excitement, it has been a whole week since he has seen his mother last, and he can't wait to tell her about the pottery project he started in art class, or the math quiz he scored a B+ on.

Nine o'clock approaches. The group grows quieter. The women gather their bags on their shoulders. Everyone is standing, facing the double glass doors, eager to see their family and friends who live behind metal bars and vibrant-colored jumpsuits. Who are ushered from cell to shower by guards with holstered guns and steel batons. And then it is as if somewhere a clock tower bellowed out announcing the ninth hour of the day. The crowd makes its way across the cement bridge and through the black-windowed entrance of the jail.

The Allegheny County Jail was opened in May of 1995 after the old Allegheny County Prison—located just miles away from the present jail—became overcrowded and structurally outdated. Each year an estimated 30,000 prisoners are booked at the jail, and of those about 20,000 prisoners are admitted for overnight or longer-term stay. Being a county jail—and not a state or federal prison—there is a constant flow of temporary inmates; recent arrests and unconvicted prisoners awaiting trial or bail.

The jail houses only 2,000 permanent or long-term inmates. The jail is organized into different pods, which are designated by number and letter and are separated into eight two-level floors. Pods are composed of inmates of the same gender and isolation level. As the city has developed, the demographics of prisoners have changed drastically.

The Allegheny County Jail Management System tracks all statistical data on booked, admitted, and long-term inmates. Each year there are an equal number of African Americans and Caucasians admitted, while other races compose about three percent of the inmate population. Male inmates predominate the prison population, making up about 80 to 85 percent of the population in a given year. The average time served is about 60 days with only four percent of the population serving a sentence longer than one year. With a smaller percentage of inmates being released every month, the jail's population has slowly been increasing to capacity.

At 10:00 a.m., the glass doors swing open, the one on the right squeaking on its hinges every time it flies back. Small groups of friends and family exit, disperse, climb into cars, unlock bike chains, reintegrate into daily city routine.

Three women coalesce around the jail's entrance and huddle around an open newspaper. One woman leans on a bent, rusted post. Above her, a dented blue sign reads BUS STOP in thick, plump letters. By her side are an empty cupcake container, an oversized black leather purse, and a large black umbrella, because this is Pittsburgh, where one moment it is clear skies and the next it is pouring rain.

"How's Rudy?" one woman asks her. Their gazes meet and before she answers the woman stands straight, pushing off the post as it violently bounces back and forth. She is short, no taller than five feet. Her long black hair is twisted tightly into a bun. She wears a Pittsburgh Steelers jersey, number 7, Ben Roethlisberger.

"Good," she begins. "Tryin' t' keep busy, says it's a lot better than New York." The other woman nods her head in response, leaning in slightly to hear the women's soft voice. "Closer to me at least," she continues. After violating the conditions of a previous arrest, her son, Rudy, is at Allegheny County Jail awaiting his court date.

"My husband's always dinging on me for comin' here. But he's family, he deserves company no matter what." She grows quiet and folds her arms across her chest.

"I know it, that's what happens," the first woman responds. "Families come divided over these things. You fight with your family 'til 'ventually, hey fuck 'em. It takes you a while to realize that the best thing you got is right around you. These people are livin' in your world." She surveys the increasingly sparse crowd around her. Her eyes are small and beady, but as she watches the people around her, her eyes are happy and the woman is calm.

"Turk's face lit up when I showed up today," the third woman says, changing the subject. She is younger and has a slight Italian accent. She wears ripped jeans, tan loafers, and an oversized army-green sweater that hangs off one of her shoulders. "Told me he's getting contracted." A shrill of excitement passes through the group as the women exchange celebratory hugs.

"I almost think that's worse," she interjects. "In here he's got friends, out here he's got nothing," the Italian woman continues, as she slides a hand through her short, blonde bangs.

"All those kids will keep 'em busy," the woman replies. The women nod in agreement and look off.

In the silence the 71B huffs its way towards the women and screeches to a stop. The women drop their tender embraces and gather their bags, jackets, and umbrellas. They silently climb the single step of the bus and take their seats, one woman in a third-row window seat, one woman clambering to the back, and the third standing at the front clinging to a thin metal railing. Moments later the bus is stopping again and the black-haired woman is starting for the door. Without any goodbyes, without a nod of the head, without any acknowledgement at all, the women exit the bus, one-by-one.

Sources:

Allegheny County Pennsylvania Public Website. History of Allegheny County Jail.
         http://www.alleghenycounty.us/jail/history.aspx Web.

Allegheny County Pennsylvania Public Website. Volume of Activity.
         http://www.alleghenycounty.us/jail/volume.aspx. Web.

Ayisha Worldenberg ayishalocoa@gmail.com
         Interviewed and observed the morning of Saturday September 14 and
         Saturday 21

William Porter willport49@mail.com
         Interviewed William and his son Austen on 10/15/2013

2009 Annual Report. Allegheny County Bureau of Corrections, Statistical Reports,
19-28.
         Retrieved from http://www.alleghenycounty.us/jail/acjail09.pdf

Homestead Triptych

Rachel Wilkinson

I.

When the Homestead Steel Strike broke out in July 1892, Andrew Carnegie was on his annual vacation. Henry Clay Frick, whom he'd hired to oversee operations at Carnegie Steel, was left to negotiate with the Amalgamated Association of Iron and Steel Workers (AA), one of the most powerful craft unions in the country. Their contract at the Homestead Steel Works was set to expire July 1 and Frick had no intention of renewing it, calling for wage reductions ranging from 22-60 percent and halting negotiations.

"We ... approve of anything you do," Carnegie wrote Frick from the remote Scottish castle where he was staying. "We are with you to the end."

On June 29, Frick fired the AA men and locked down the steel mill. Though the union represented only 700 of the 3800 mill workers, every worker went on strike.

A political cartoon at this time shows a caricatured Carnegie sitting atop the Homestead Works: he is fat, with muttonchops and a pinstripe suit, smoking a cigar while cracking a whip, and lounging on bags upon bags of money. Carnegie Steel had brought in some of the largest profits in recorded history—$4.5 million in the six months before the strike, $119 billion today. "Was there ever such a business!" Carnegie had exclaimed.

In response to the strike, Frick built a "baronial castle" with 10-foot high fence and barbed wire to keep workers out of the closed mill. The July 3, 1892, newspaper article accompanying the Carnegie cartoon describes the construction of "Fort Frick," as it was nicknamed by Homesteaders.

On July 4, Frick wrote to Carnegie, "The newspapers, as usual, are inclined toward the enemy, and doubtless will raise a great howl when they discover that we have the audacity to attempt to guard and protect our property." Escalating things further, workers militarized the town, establishing eight-hour watch-shifts of the mill and patrolling the bordering Monongahela River. By July 5, it had been a five-day standoff with no end in sight.

The next day, Frick sent for 300 Pinkerton National Detectives, a mercenary army known for strikebreaking, infiltrating unions and violently intimidating workers. When they arrived by river barge at 4 a.m. on July 6, Frick had hoped they would be able to sneak ashore and simply take back the mill. He would reopen it using non-union labor and go right back into production. But the strikers, still on watch, saw the Pinkertons coming and blew the mill whistle, drawing out 10,000 people in Homestead.

They rose from their beds and raced down to the riverbank. Many of them were armed with Civil War rifles, shotguns, pistols; others brandished sticks, stones, and clubs made by prying apart fence boards. In minutes, they tore down the barbed wire fence surrounding the mill and overtook it, facing down the Pinkertons. A few townspeople threw rocks at the Pinkertons, but the strikers told them to hold off. The crowd shouted and warned the Pinkertons not to step off the barge, but they did.

It's unclear which side fired first. The Pinkertons had Winchester rifles. Strikers tried to set their barges on fire. They threw dynamite. They tried to fire an antique cannon. They launched flaming rafts onto the water. They poured oil into the river, hoping to light a slick such that it would burst into flames. Though eyewitnesses from both sides confirm the initial firefight lasted about 10 minutes, shooting continued intermittently for hours until the Pinkertons surrendered at 5 p.m. Finally allowed to come ashore, they were beaten by angry workers, then escorted to jail in the Homestead Opera House, and sent back to Pittsburgh the next morning. Four days later, at Frick's request, the Pennsylvania gover-nor called in 8,000 state militiamen to restore peace.

In the months following, 100 workers were charged with treason and the AA fell apart. By November 1892, workers agreed to longer hours and Carnegie and Frick's reduced wages. Carnegie's year-end prof-its rose to $106 million—today, $280 billion—while he called Home-stead the greatest regret of his life.

"It was so unnecessary," Carnegie wrote in reply to a sympathetic note a few weeks after the strike. "The Works are not worth one drop of human blood. I wish they had sunk."

II.

There are different counts of how many people died during the Homestead Strike. Some put the casualties at nine strikers and three Pinkertons; others only seven Pinkertons; others only seven strikers, as on the state historical marker at the battle site. In the archives at the Uni-versity of Pittsburgh, there are seven steelworker inquest files from the Allegheny County Coroner's Office.

The seven workers' inquests are stored with three Pinkertons', all of them stacked together in the same blue file box since they were ac-quired in 1982—five years before the Homestead Steel Works officially closed. Most reports appear on an official Coroner's form, but some are just written out in longhand on loose-leaf notebook paper.

Medico-legal language was becoming standardized at the begin-ning of the twentieth century, so the reports have the same impartial tone we associate with high-profile cases: *Joe Soppa, age 40 (?), occupation: mill hand, suffering from symptoms of shock due to a gunshot wound of the left knee joint; injuries received at 5 am, Tuesday, July 6, 1892 at Homestead. John Morris, 28, shot in forehead during riot. Henry Streiger, 19, shot in neck during riot. JW Klein [no age] shot on barge.* There is, of course, very little context.

Adjacent to the Homestead Strike site on the Monongahela Riv-er sits a 68-foot labyrinth. A 2009 memorial by artist Lorraine Vullo, the labyrinth is a walkable series of winding passageways, with a single path leading inward toward its center. It's cut cleanly into the grass, the river-front since cleared of rocks. 250 triangular stones line its perimeter, all bearing names of steelmaking sites in Western Pennsylvania, including

Carnegie Steel Mill. The plaque at the site notes the historical import of labyrinths—their "signification of new meanings and purposes" for thousands of years.

According to Vullo, the intricate design of the Homestead Labyrinth was inspired by medieval labyrinths, which appeared on the floors of cathedrals. The maze-like quality of the labyrinths was supposed to evoke the idea of pilgrimage. In the 17th century, it's said some worshippers in Chartres Cathedral followed its labyrinthine path while praying on their knees. In all labyrinths, there are no dead ends or wrong turns, but the only way out of their intricate pathways is going all the way through them.

The Homestead Labyrinth takes about 20 minutes to walk, curling in parallel paths to the circle's center, then back out along the circle's edge in a configuration that is dizzying. Across the street from the labyrinth on Waterfront Drive is U.S. Steel's Research and Technology Center. It's a high-tech, LEED-certified, green building, which its corporate website notes is located a site "once occupied by the company's historic Homestead Works."

III.

It's now difficult to imagine 10,000 people rioting in Homestead, where the site of the Steel Works is a 260-acre shopping complex called The Waterfront. It's is a mixture of upscale restaurants and shops arranged on an "old-fashioned village square," and big box stores. Among them is Target, which in March 2014 released an anti-union video called "Think Hard: Protect Your Signature" for its minimum-wage employees. The video warns that retail is "a competitive business," urging workers to think twice about organized labor, as it would change Target's "fast, fun and friendly culture."

An online travel guide to the Waterfront reminds the reader that huge brick smokestacks, still intact at one of the complex's entrances, are one of the only remnants of Homestead's former steel mill—which, while giving the Waterfront character, also makes it easy to spot.

The Heart of Saturday Night

Kyle Mimnaugh

You are driving. As you are jarred out of your state of highway hypnosis, familiar fluorescent green signs bombard your eyes. You wipe the haze away to read, "Pittsburgh." You are home; or you might just be passing through. Either way, the name of this city evokes many emotions and preconceived ideas. Some true, some false. Many people who have not been keeping up with the progression of this city imagine it to be something along the lines of current Detroit or a scene from *The Warriors.* Neither is true. Pittsburgh has a rich, complicated history that it does not shy away from. When you are here, you feel an overwhelming, almost palpable, sense of nostalgia. No matter where you look, you can see the Pittsburgh of old encroaching on the new.

The country's "Most Livable City" is known for steel. As well as the Steelers, the Penguins, the Pirates, the "yinz," and the "n'at." And as far as the rest of the country is concerned, that is it. I am not from Pittsburgh, I will admit that. I am a recent transplant from New Jersey by way of South Carolina. I went from the hustle and bustle of living in shadow of New York City to getting excited about the postal worker showing up with whatever package I may have ordered from Amazon three to five days earlier (the South can be that mind numbing). Against my family's wishes, I went to film school. I majored in Media Arts, a fancy name for film and television production with just a smattering of graphic design. I minored in Film Studies just to make sure I was com-

61

pletely unemployable after college. After many years of stagnating in the 300 percent humidity of South Carolina, I decided to pack my bags and move to Pittsburgh on a whim. It was one of the wisest decisions I have ever made. This city welcomed me with open arms and did not give two shits where I came from or what I was doing here.

Being a film buff and living in the South, I sometimes had to drive absurd distances just to see a film I wanted to watch, which is ridiculous. But if your name does not rhyme with Schmichael Schmay, your little indie micro-budget film does not get distribution to the mainstream theaters in the south. Now I can close my eyes, spin around ten times, point in any given direction and drive to a theater playing exactly what I want to watch.

For being considered such a "little big city," there are a lot of theaters in Pittsburgh. Just about every large corporate chain you can think of is here, but it also has a shocking amount of "art house" theaters and even drive-ins. There are over two dozen theaters just within a 25-mile radius of where I live; the theaters range from large multiplexes to small, one-screen theaters. You have your local staples like The Waterfront, boasting twenty-two screens. You also have your smaller, more niche places like Row House Cinema and The Hollywood Theater in Dormont.

These places are dying out, but they remain important neighborhood staples. These theaters are the cultural trendsetters for the subsequent surrounding shops, restaurants, and galleries that may spring up around them. Theaters like The Hollywood take the typically passive experience of film-going, and make it an almost holy experience. They force you to be a part of the film. They encourage you to have a dialogue about the film you just watched. They have movie and TV show-themed events where one can let their inner film nerd flag fly. One of the most interesting attractions they have at The Hollywood is their live music supporting classic silent films. Practices like these are more immersive than any 3D/4D garbage corporate Hollywood wants to stuff down our throats.

One thing all the theaters in Pittsburgh have in common, no matter how big or small, is the fact that they all play classic films. Pittsburgh is the only city I have been to that has theaters like Row House Cinema and The Oaks Theater, which ditch mainstream Hollywood fare and fill their time slots with films that are not necessarily huge blockbusters, but are cult classics.

Downtown's Harris Theater recently ran a "Polish Masterpiece Series" curated by Martin Scorsese, something I could imagine being on the IFC channel at home, but not in a theater. Row House just had a showcase of Tim Burton films in their "Tim Burton Directs" series, something they did recently with the films of Stanley Kubrick. One of my favorite places to see a film in Pittsburgh is The Manor Theater in Squirrel Hill. This theater has managed to somehow evolve, stay relevant, and thrive after being open for over 90 years. It is also a place where a stranger asks you what your favorite part of the film you just watched was, while washing your hands after expelling that eight dollar small soda you just slurped down. All of that being said, one has to ask themselves, is this really just nostalgia for the films and days of old, or is it the people of Pittsburgh's inability to let go of the past?

Pittsburgh is part of the Rust Belt. In other words, once industry left this area so did the people and the money. This is the Pittsburgh people know. This city was in a downward spiral for many years, until new life was pumped into the city like the smoke stacks lining the skyline. Companies returned back into Pittsburgh. Creative types like me moved here and gentrified the hell out of the place, shining a spotlight on the culture that never really went anywhere, but was just covered in soot and bad publicity. Aside from new industry and technology making its way back to Pittsburgh, so did film. Big Hollywood films like *The Dark Knight Rises* and *Jack Reacher* were shot here for its chameleon-like landscapes and enticing tax breaks.

The roots of film are embedded deep in Pittsburgh. It is somewhere where it would not be out of place for even the most weathered looking, gum-crackin' "Yinzer" to say his favorite film is something along the lines of *Casablanca*. There are so many moving parts to this city. It has an undeniable rhythm to it; almost as if Busby Berkeley himself is directing the whole city and all of its denizens in a gorgeous, albeit very gray, dance number.

So why does Pittsburgh place so much emphasis on old films? Why do its citizens forego seeing the newest Hollywood blockbuster, to see a replaying of a classic like *The Godfather*? Why do the classic films shown around here, especially at theaters like the Waterfront, go on sale months in advance and sell out almost as soon as they are available? It is because these films serve as a celluloid time capsule to a time long forgotten elsewhere in the United States. A simpler time. A time where people built things with their hands. A time where going to see a movie was a sacred practice, and not just something you did in between mall shopping and picking up your dry cleaning. One may go to church on Sunday, but Saturday belonged to the cinema.

Not everyone here is a Carnegie. People came from humble beginnings and they appreciated what they had; they were practical and accepted hand-me-downs not with disdain, but with appreciation and gratitude. Pittsburghers of old had the "if it ain't broke, don't fix it" mentality ingrained in them from an early age. A friend of mine told me about a time not too long ago when a midnight showing of a film kept selling out in every theater. However, they only had one print of the film, so they rigged the projectors in each theater to feed into each other and play in multiple theaters simultaneously. Now that is what I call ingenuity.

Re-purposing things is huge in Pittsburgh. In other areas of the United States, if a building was old and crumbling, it would be torn down and a new structure would take its place. If someone wanted to open up a new coffee shop, store, or indie theater, they would slap a new coat of paint on the sucker and call it a day. Look at the old twenty-two screen Loews Multiplex in North Versailles. When it filed for bankruptcy and closed in 2001, it wasn't left vacant for time to take its toll. It turned into an oddball community of vendors from all over the greater Pittsburgh are, who hock their wares every Saturday and Sunday. When the old Warner Theater in downtown Pittsburgh closed after 65 years of playing films like Douglas Fairbanks's *Headin' South* in 1918, and *Flashdance* in 1983, it wasn't left to be a vacant façade in an otherwise vibrant cityscape. It was turned into a place where ex-cons could get fresh clothes and a new start. We reuse things here. Everything is beautiful, everything has a purpose, nothing is beyond saving.

Time Capsule, 2005

Robert Yune

Pittsburgh. Steel city. Iron City (beer). Distance from Morgantown, West Virginia: 78 miles. Pittsburgh, the "Paris of the Appalachians." Distance from Paris, France: 3,987 miles.

True story: she grabbed her bottom lip and pulled it to the side. "Heah," she said, pointing. She had the Steelers logo tattooed on her gums. She let go, rubbing her face. "Just wanted to be true to my roots." The Steelers don't have cheerleaders—what's the point?

Pittsburgh: 80 days of sunlight a year. Andy Warhol had to flee to sunny New York. The Warhol Museum downtown has a fully stocked bar—it's the first thing you see when you walk through the door. Their happy hour sucks.

Working steel mills in Pittsburgh: The imposing Edgar Thomson plant in Braddock, the Irvin Works plant in Dravosburg, the Clairton coke plant, the U.S. Steel plant in the Mon Valley. How many does your city have?

Oakland is a busy neighborhood in east Pittsburgh, a "cultural district" that contains a business district, three universities, residential neighborhoods and several hospitals, all crammed into half a square mile. Hospitals. There are 5,759 hospitals in the United States and most of them are in Oakland, situated amidst a maze of one-way streets and conveniently located atop one of the steepest hills in the nation—Pitt students call it "Cardiac Hill" as they pant their way to Trees Hall. Let's pour out some liquor for the old stadium before we roll downhill. The new stadium—sorry, "events center"—looks like an Austrian Museum of Banking.

Downhill to the Cathedral of Learning. In the 1920s, Chancellor Bowman commissioned the structure, prompting workers and students to call it "Bowman's erection." No one knows why it was built: I like to picture Chancellor Bowman enjoying the panoramic view of Oakland from his castle-like mansion overlooking the city. *You know what this area needs?* he says to no one in particular. *A thirty-six floor gothic skyscraper.* He throws his snifter of brandy on his lead crystal window, watches a tall amber stain run drip onto Forbes Avenue, the new axis upon which Oakland would turn. He turns and pulls his robe tight around his chest. *We'll begin tomorrow.*

"Spare some change? Spare some change?" Shake your head and the beggar, a skinny man in a dirty blue bomber jacket, will move on. A few feet and you can't even hear him. Amidst the sound of the bus's massive diesel engine, there are blaring horns muted through the windows. "Aw hell no," the man stuck in traffic says into his cell phone. "Goddamn Pitt students." Indeed. It's Arrival Survival week, meaning a swarm of bright-eyed Pitt freshmen are descending upon Oakland. They push their belongings in giant yellow carts, laundromat-sized, with PITT HOUSING stamped on the side. One student has his filled entirely with ramen noodles. And then there's the usual: computers, clothes, vacuum cleaners, fans, mini-refrigerators. As the traffic inches by, you spot a freshman girl pushing a cart filled to the top with stuffed animals.

"Got any change, change?" Meet Sombrero Man, one of Oakland's many panhandlers. His broad, dirty face is shaded by an authentic-looking straw sombrero. Occasionally, freshmen steal his hat and hang it like a trophy outside their dorm windows. He always gets a new one, though. No one knows from where.

Sombrero Man's on the move, and so are we. It's a dense neighborhood—this entire tour only covers about four blocks. Now we're passing another Oakland landmark: Diplodocus carnegii, the huge bronze dinosaur outside the Carnegie Museum of Art. It's tall and as long as a school bus, its thin neck stretching to overlook Forbes Avenue.

Oh yeah. This happens a lot during Arrival Survival—and here, you thought it was just a clever rhyme. There's a poorly marked intersection where Forbes Avenue changes from being a two-way street and abruptly becomes a one-way. If you don't turn down a side street, you face the very real prospect of a head-on collision with four lanes of oncoming traffic. Next to this intersection is the Carnegie Museum of Natural History. It's a huge stone building adorned with statues: bronze Copernicus and Shakespeare guard the entrance. From the roof, statues of great pioneers and architects gaze down pitilessly at the scene below. A minivan stops in the middle of this trap/intersection. Horns blare. As it attempts a K-turn, a few cars speed around it.

Speaking of transportation, there's one last thing I'd like to show you—"Excuse me, excuse me," a young man in a red shirt says, interrupting me. He runs ahead of us, facing us and walking backwards. "Please, my man," he says to me. He's in his early twenties, with a scraggly mustache and a neon green baseball hat. We stop. I exhale in disgust. "My car broke down on the Boulevard of the Allies yesterday."

"Sorry," I say.

"It's out of the shop, I mean they're done with it in the shop— you know the Exxon down there—and anyways I need it to get to work." I tell him I don't have any money. "Come on," he says, looking at you, pleading. He says there's four grand worth of tools in the back. He can repay you. His inflection is so perfect, his eyes pleading. He could be faking, or is that genuine sorrow behind the "I'm ashamed I have to ask" tone? That look in his eyes…one can't fake that, right?

Enough. I say something rude to him and walk away. You look back at the man—maybe you're even wondering if you have any ones or fives. He's good. And maybe he's telling the truth. Either way, that's the third time his car has broken down this week.

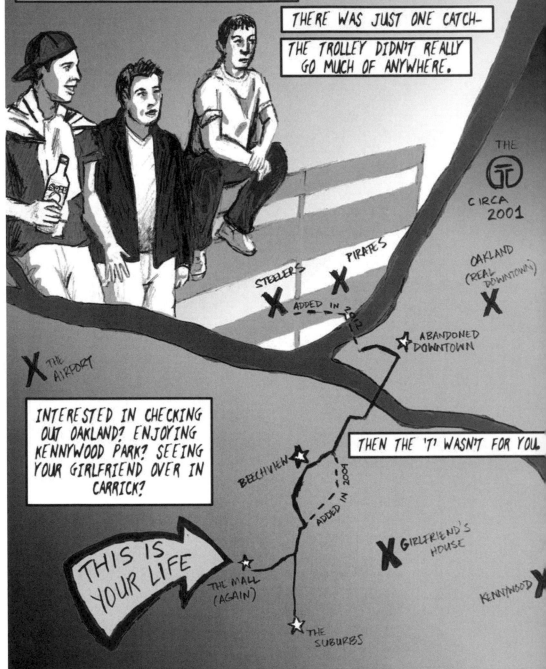

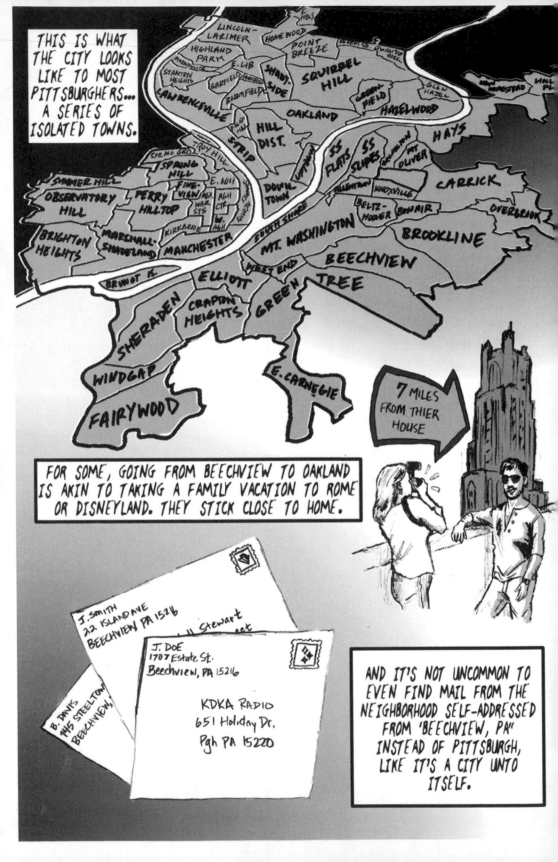

THIS IS WHAT THE CITY LOOKS LIKE TO MOST PITTSBURGHERS... A SERIES OF ISOLATED TOWNS.

7 MILES FROM THIER HOUSE

FOR SOME, GOING FROM BEECHVIEW TO OAKLAND IS AKIN TO TAKING A FAMILY VACATION TO ROME OR DISNEYLAND. THEY STICK CLOSE TO HOME.

AND IT'S NOT UNCOMMON TO EVEN FIND MAIL FROM THE NEIGHBORHOOD SELF-ADDRESSED FROM 'BEECHVIEW, PA" INSTEAD OF PITTSBURGH, LIKE IT'S A CITY UNTO ITSELF.

Retraced Route

Adam Dupaski

T*he Akron Hound counter rep* answers the bus is on time as far as he knows, yes. Take a seat: neck tattoo with Cleveland snapback stares from the pay phone, busted nose with slicked hair tells XXL coat he just got out of jail, Kangol hat hands over $5 for a stack of DVD-Rs, tweaker sweatpants wanders with a Taco Bell bag.

The driver's name is Janek, in his fluorescent green vest; he'll only warn anyone once who starts cussing or getting loud on the phone. After wishing everyone a good ride, he jokes that Pittsburgh, it's ok, but he loves Cleveland and he's glad to be moving so he can get back there tonight. Tells young earring'ed driver-in-training in the front seat he's from Slovakia originally, and his son is a cop. Greyhound called him at midnight to take this route, he's been working seven or eight days straight. Across the aisle, two ladies share a can of Vienna sausages and say they're heading home to North Carolina and are they on the right bus? 76 to Youngstown, cornfields, snow melting, oddly warm and bright. Ham with muenster cheese and mustard, necessary Hound sustenance, just like Mark leaving out of Cleveland with a sandwich your mother had made him, for years after he described how slowly he savored the texture on his ride to Binghamton. But taking a sandwich out of your bag nowadays, especially one thin and wrapped in foil, that locates your memory on a slow train between Kraków and Rzeszów.

Pull into Youngstown right across from the Mahoning County

Jail, no break cause you're running late but some get off to smoke and Blackhawks cap comes back in saying the Hound from Detroit to Akron had no heat so this is great. Follow the hills peripherally and soon you're barreling into the Burgh over that high Allegheny, all those bridges (your favorite the 10th Street: Aztec Gold or simple yellow?), always construction and detours, all that brown and grey and slight evergreen glimpsed through the truss of the Birmingham Bridge, too much sun on brick, a city with weight yet never without its smog comfort and iron-bound charm. The station is a few blocks from where you did data entry while listening to Howard Stern and Rye Coalition, where you never got up the nerve to ask out that co-worker who had a big burn scar on her face.

Retrace the route to the city where you once lived, the route to the friend with whom you lived, after all. Pittsburgh: the city has become the friend, but whatever memory it admits is but a momentary thaw before further calcification. City-as-friend and friend-as-city are hidden now more than during the visit but less than when you inhabited the place, with so much unforgotten. The Burgh is not of your youth, but of a more trying age and so there it remains, all the more likely to prod and provoke. As the mnemonics self-defeat, movement along the route is pulled towards a more collaborative forgetting. This movement—the first level of memory and further establishments of forgetting—all that occurred close to a year ago now.

Billy picks you up in a dusty black Nissan and immediately has to make three U-turns to get towards the correct on-ramp. Across the river is the Warhol where you saw Nobukazu Takemura with John Herndon on drums, and you'd imitate Jean-Paul Belmondo in the basement photo-booth. Soon you're heading into Oakland, there's Joe Mama's, ever-corny, so many Friday evenings started there, Billy wearing his Rock Hudson sweater, you tried to become *regulars* as if that was possible at a place like that, one Monday even calling off work to buy used Shostakovich vinyl nearby and then consider Joe Mama's for a martini lunch, but that seemed ridiculous and you got falafel instead.

Park on Filmore and walk down to Caliban's to be confronted with those same shelves of *Evergreen Review* and old New Directions: Beckett, Corso, and Genet haven't moved much. Billy puts one knee on the floor to examine HD's *Tribute to Freud* while you find *The Polish Peasant in Europe and America* and tell him you're going to read passages of it aloud to your father when you get home. With tax it comes to $8.02, hand over a tenner and say you have no pennies, you're given a pile of change anyway cause this isn't the kind of place with a take-a-penny-leave-a-penny. Walk past where a video store used to be, remember renting Varda's *The Gleaners and I* there upon first moving to the city, and continue to a coffee shop where they have a Jolly Rancher pop selection, a rather shocking product but here you are back in America, back in Pittsburgh. Order a chai tea and immediately regret it cause there's so much milk, end up putting all the loose change from the *Polish Peasant* purchase in the tip jar anyway right when goatee eyebrow-ring turns around, a real Costanza situation, one bad decision after another. Billy drinks his coffee black, you ask about his father who is nearing retirement and what he'll do with his time, he used to drive all over TX and OK and AR for work so maybe he'll just keep cruising round while listening to his favorite smooth jazz stations with names like *The Wave* and *Breeze*.

A quick cruise through Shadyside past the crepe shop on Filbert where you both worked flipping crepes with soytang or whipped cream and pushing Belgian mineral water, Stereolab droning on the stereo while in between customers you wrote the script for the Lucky Situationist: a dance scene modeled on *Band of Outsiders*, a nod to the Nim game in *Last Year at Marienbad* (so long ago, that Francophile phase), a street fight in which you're choked with mandarin oranges. Filmed it all between Filbert and the apartment on South Atlantic, showed it at Pittsburgh Filmmakers for Billy's final show, your mother still watches it to see your starring role. Continue on South Aiken, down which you walked one gloomy Sunday in the snow for lack of anything better to do and ran into absolutely nothing of interest, a failed walk if there is such a thing, no less a nearly failed memory.

Up South Atlantic past where you lived on the top floor, that slob of a landlord Julio tried to cheat you out of your deposit when you moved out, looks surprisingly rundown now but while living there you called it the Palace. Two lefts past the corner store that used to be a 7-Eleven and somehow had a legal bar in the back, local fans sipping Iron City and Bud tallboys slowly, and then the beat back of the house down Asterisk Way where the two old ladies from the ground floor would put out a kiddie pool for splashing around on the weekends and Shakes would come over, old but wiry with stubble and huge glasses in athletic shorts, a booming voice, he'd whoop it up with them. Who else lived there: a friendly long-hair with a huge metal and hardcore record collection, a West Virginian who always wanted to sell you Vicodin and whose son stole his grandma's car to peel round back early one morning, later that day he got arrested.

"Welcome to Friendship" now up Stratford Ave. to the other apartment, the library where you'd smoke corncob pipes from Rite Aid while watching Bergman films, read Studs Terkel's *Working* in the bath, leave "In the Air Tonight" on repeat, and on the porch be asked questions endlessly by Alik, who Billy says lives in NC and either owns or works in a textile factory, both astonishing propositions. As you enter rush-hour traffic along Penn Ave. the memory frameworks come more quickly: Jasmine, Jesse, Janelle, David, Rick, PhD, Terry, Hot Cup of Soup and the waitress from the Squirrel Hill Cafe with the dyed bright red hair, watching Sun Ra's *Space Is the Place* at Ed's apartment, feeling like you ordered the wrong kind of beer at the Sharp Edge, driving out to the North Hills and always returning with a sense of disappointment, dancing with Hot Cup of Soup at Gooski's (to something on the jukebox: "Holiday in Cambodia"?), buying your first Fela Kuti record at Paul's CDs, an arm wrestling competition at a Garfield Artworks opening, rattlesnake pierogi at the Church Brew Works. But Billy says he doesn't like to encounter people he knew from back then too much, like Jim, who he ran into in front of Spice Island in Oakland, the guy hadn't aged at all, he used to deliver flowers, you ask if he still dresses like he's in the Strokes.

Now to Giant Eagle for some Great Lakes Christmas Ale and snacks, spend a while goofing on difficult chips-and-salsa choices before deciding on Tostito's "cantina-style" all around, then drive the 30 yards to the state store where you check the vodka selection even though you brought a gift bottle of ☐liwowica and they have nothing of interest anyway, no good Polish vods and you know American ☐ubrówka is a poor heavy-chemical substitute. Billy wants to buy some Scotch, he mentions Dewar's which brings you back to the second-floor of the Zephyr in Kent, a double Dewar's kept the couple repetitions of "Sister Ray" you'd put on the jukebox tolerable but it's still a nauseous recall, so he gets a bottle of Woodford Reserve instead which no one ends up touching that night, and the next morning he puts it on his liquor cabinet next to a bottle of Pimm's and when you ask why he has Pimm's, he says he doesn't know.

Back in the Nissan, you head for more beer at D's Six Pax and Dogz, where Billy parks in an awkward though legal spot across the street and you jaywalk confusedly but this place is supposed to be good, they do vegan dogs too, which is always the first thing you recall about Toronto, the street vendors selling vegan hot dogs. Cut back to the beer cave and pick out a few choice bottles, none of which you sample that night, and then drive past the Regent Square Cinema where you both saw *Le Cercle Rouge* some rainy Sunday night and another time watched Lee Ranaldo and Text of Light play to the films of Stan Brakhage, which were amazing on the big screen but the drummer played his snare upside down and picked at the snares like he was deboning a fish, you're still not sure about his style.

Finally to Billy's place, which looks like some sort of low-slung lodge but more Tudor than Ohiopyle, and inside it's all crown molding and beams and prints of Proust, (maybe) Stendhal, birds, Napoleon's death mask, steamships, and books on Baldessari, cave art, the Prado, used copies of *War and War* and *A Minor Apocalypse* acquired on your tip, plenty of old New Directions and *Evergreen Review* from Caliban's, a photo of Ray and you from a previous visit when Billy lived on Liberty Ave. back in Bloomfield, a bust of Lincoln. You meet Eve formally before settling in to drinking Great Lakes at the dining room table, break open the cantina with whispered exclamations of whew and a lot of head shaking as if it's some local delicacy, and then you present the ☐ liwowica, which is taken slowly with expressions of burn while you pet the cats whose names you never found out.

On the tour of the kitchen, you are shown the cheese paper Billy bought for Eve as a "gift" because she claimed he wrapped cheese improperly, and you all look out the window at the nearby Episcopalian church, which they describe as basically chill with a nice red door. In another two hours you are given the tour upstairs, there is an old Penguin paperback of *Against Nature* on Billy's night table, in his office you peruse the shelves of ontology and film theory, and you would joke the next morning about the difficulty of being an ontological subject, which you both knew was misguided and lame. Get a quick conversation going about techné and how the cats are not allowed in his office, soon realizing it's getting late and no one has mentioned dinner yet, which is to be a delicious pasta with three kinds of cheese and a salad with radicchio, you go for seconds realizing it could be a heavy night like that time you wolfed down the Parmageddon (grilled cheese with kraut and pierogi) sandwich at Melt in Lakewood with Ray and Hans, woke up at 3 a.m. on a west-side couch with a horrible gut anchor sinking you into sweat and headache, and later that day Hans took you to a professional wrestling match at the amphitheater by the Cuyahoga. After dinner Eve offers you a "sweet bite" in the form of a caramel, which she pronounces pleasantly with three syllables, and eventually you even dip back into the cantina, why not. Before going to sleep you all spend ten minutes using extreme force to pull out a mattress stuffed into the corner of the closet, working up a sweat, socked feet slipping over the carpet.

There are three options for coffee in the morning: a regular machine, Keurig, and French press (your choice). Rifle about for some bread to make toast and eat a banana, your workday breakfast, and soon Billy is up figuring out which coffee device to use. He makes more white toast and offers you some, you accept but then start talking about how tasty the pasta the previous night was, so you pull it out of the fridge and sample it while both figuring that although it's excellent cold you might as well heat it up, so Billy gets it sizzling and then uses the toast, that earlier breakfast concept, to soak up the oil after the cheese is all hot and gooey and you do the same, whipping the sullied bread into the overflowing rubbish can before settling at the dining room table to once again eat pasta, this time silently. When done you sit back with an actual gut anchor and not just the memory thereof, quickly ill to talk about how ill you feel, and it is quiet except for a couple exasperated *whews* until you retire to the back porch so Billy can have a square and you sit there in a stupor watching the snow melt.

After discussing how you may throw up, you leave for a walk around one of those dour Pittsburgh neighborhoods of dark, chimneyed brick houses and there's rain in the air as you amble up the hill chatting about technical writing as well as teaching business communication and what that means for studies of violence and rhetoric (nothing good, it turns out), then cut to the left and venture under the busway, take a couple photos before returning to the lodge so they can pack for their trip to Ohio, and you settle down for a quick pre-lunch nap as a result of all the three-cheese breakfast pasta and walking.

By the time they're ready to go it's raining, suitable conditions for a Pittsburgh exit, and after you get into the backseat next to the two cat-carriers, Billy puts on the Schubert piano works that you'll listen to for the entire car trip back to Ohio, Schubert played at low volume with a sheen of driving, rain, and chatter over top. An hour and a half later you stop at the Mahoning Valley service plaza for a bite and you could really go for a slice of Sbarro's 'cause that's ideal rest stop fare and didn't there used to be one here? But the only choices are Panera and Dairy Queen so Billy jokes about getting the DQ fried shrimp basket, an unfortunate idea any time, and you head wearily over to Panera to order an overpriced "artisanal" smoked turkey panini then sit watching a bleak Friday afternoon scene of rain and passing cars on the turnpike, catch sight of an overweight woman at the DQ counter with her sweatpants falling below her rear-end and that is so awful you decide not to look over at DQ again, perhaps ever, and after returning to the car you doze to the Schubert and rain while you are driven home. In the driveway you say goodbye rather quickly, though you probably should have encouraged them to come in and say hi to your parents but they wanted to get going anyway. Your mother opens the door so you chat, eat a few Christmas cookies, and then retire upstairs to watch the rain turn into snow.

Pittsburgh: lived there for a year and a half, and via Kraków and Ohio, you continue retracing the route of forgetting through its streets.

The Lonesome Passing of Jay Paulson

Andy Kohler

*I*n 2010, I was the singer/guitarist in an indie rock band out of Youngstown and we played half a dozen shows in Pittsburgh. These trips were mini-voyages for me; two of the guys in the band lived in Youngstown, so the trip was only an hour for them, but for me and Scott, it was more like two hours from Portage County. We didn't mind; we'd been friends since second grade and were eager to have the time to talk.

The night drives amazed me, to think of how far we were traveling just to play for an hour for some people that didn't know who we were or that we were even coming. We'd hurtle along the freeways, heading southeast, the land growing into hills, the dark hills dotted with the lights of unseen houses.

The Pittsburgh I found in 2010 was full of characters, people like me making art, but they were pushing their boundaries like it was life and death. All of the old factories had long gone silent. The old warehouses were being built into studios; the steel workers' descendants were being reshaped into artists and thinkers. They were wilder, more independent, had been on their own for years, were scared of nothing. They were younger than me.

And then there was Jay Paulson, a guitarist our age who we met on "Myspace." Jay was quiet, with what my sister described as a strange aura about him. He was never excited or engaged. If you talked to him, he just sort of nodded and said, "Fer sure.. Fer sure..." Over and over.

He slipped around like a shadow. I never saw him with a close friend, just relaxing and looking human. He had that tired, jaundiced attitude people get when they've been disappointed over and over.

He looked like some notorious 1960s rock singer, with dark volatile eyes, short beard and shoulder length black curly hair. You'd think he could walk into a room and command a presence, but if you looked in his eyes they were muddy, disturbing, unreadable. In cold weather, he wore a long coat and strode around, and though he was easily overlooked in a crowd, you could feel Jay in the room like a radio broadcasting a broken signal. He was a man self-isolated in pain, so singularly focused on an unlikely goal of fame that he seemingly couldn't communicate with nor relate to anyone.

And yet, he was a goof. If he'd laughed at himself more, he might have been lovable. The first show we played with his band, he forgot his guitar. I let him borrow mine, but he had trouble tuning it. He finally got it to where he wanted it, but his vibe had been thrown off. He was upset. While he played his set, he ignored the audience and looked at himself in the mirrors around the stage. The Bloomfield Saloon was basically a sports bar with a stage, and most people were watching hockey or talking. Jay didn't get much of a reaction and he seemed unhappy. After his set, he sat down behind me at a table with a woman and they talked but she suddenly got mad and stomped out on him.

We felt sorry for the guy. He was just starting out, and we tried to include him in shows. Often when he played, his guitar would have a string slightly out of tune, or his singing wasn't great. People didn't listen for long. I started wishing we could play with someone else, somebody who might attract some listeners rather than drive them away, but since I wasn't organizing the shows, I had no real say.

Jay brought a large entourage to their next show, which this time was at a bar on Carson Street in Pittsburgh. I was initially impressed by how many people came to see him, but as his band played I realized that the group, most notably a few drunk girls, were making fun of him. He seemed to not notice; once or twice he chuckled embarrassedly, but the rest of the time he tried to ignore them. The weird sadness of it struck me and I stayed there, glued to my seat by a combination of lethargy and loyalty. I just wished he would play something good and blow everyone away, make us all believers. The funny thing about Jay's original songs is that they were either poppy love songs or hard-rocking party songs, with these inane lyrics about relaxing and letting go. He'd even made a few semi-professional videos of his originals, and the only actor in the videos who didn't seem to be believing the lyrics and having fun was Jay. While the other actors laughed and danced and sprayed beer on one another, Jay seemed somber and unhappy. The irony was unintentional and cringe-worthy.

While I watched Jay's band, a group of people who were leaving stopped by and complimented me on my band's previous set. As Jay played, one person said to me, "This music is terrible, why are you sitting here listening to it?" And without thinking, I said, "This is our friend." But he wasn't really. I was just embarrassed that the guys in my band had all left and were outside smoking or getting food, and I felt sorry for the guy. I never saw Jay again after that. I'd just see his show listings from time to time on the internet. In time, my band broke up and I stopped making trips to Pittsburgh.

I would have forgotten about Jay entirely except that one night in December 2013, I got a Facebook message from a bandmate with a link to a "breaking news update" that said a man had been shot and killed by police in a Pittsburgh suburb. It was Jay. Video footage showed the front yard at night surrounded by yellow police tape and the swirling lights of cop cars. Police officers were filmed putting evidence into boxes.

In the next couple days, a few articles came out with new information. Apparently, late one night Jay had taken a .38 pistol to his ex-girlfriend's new boyfriend's house. The man was outside stringing up Christmas lights. Jay apparently said to the man, "We're going for a ride." Instead they went inside the house. The guy pleaded for his life. Jay insisted the guy call his girlfriend and break up with her. The guy escaped into the basement and crawled out a window and called 911. Jay came out the front door and a newly arrived police officer ordered him to drop his gun. Instead, Jay fired at the cop. The cop shot at Jay six times, hitting him in the legs. Forty-three minutes later, at the hospital Jay was declared dead.

For six days, there wasn't any new information. A few web searches revealed that in the past, Jay had been charged with criminal mischief, loitering, and prowling. I also found that his dad had died a few years back, and discovered old videos of him on YouTube as an adolescent trying to do tricks on a skateboard. Jay would be falling down concrete steps, making a theatrical pratfall, trying to catch himself, showing off bloody arm wounds and scrapes, and faux-crying for the ever whirling camera. Sometimes he'd even be laying facedown on the ground after a fall and not getting up or moving. He wore a sweat-soaked T-shirt, torn jeans. Finally, a silent vignette where a stoic youngster, maybe six years old, looks uncomfortable with hands in pants pockets as Jay tries to entice him to try the skateboard. The kid looks at Jay's ripped pants and bloody elbows and the message is clear: this youngster considers Jay crazy and his injuries inexplicable.

A final news article came out: the autopsy found that the bullet that had killed Jay, the one in his head, came from his own gun. When the full details of the story came out, neighbors were interviewed through locked screen doors and expressed relief that it hadn't been a random home invasion; that there was some logic to the crime and that it was decisively over.

And that was it—all of Jay's innocuous attempts to make music finished for good, his silver Chevy Impala no longer needed. All those things—his self-made videos, his pictures on Facebook and MySpace smiling with friends, dark photos on Pittsburgh streets, photos from sunny days on the water somewhere, all different hairstyles, but the same Jay face. Underneath his mild brown-eyed glance was the grit, the resignation and struggle, locked in immutable attempts to break out of himself and his ordinary life, and now at the morgue, either his eyes were open in one last gaze or his eyes were closed in final sleep. He died in the snow, he was shot in the legs and maybe he knew he'd be going to jail for a long time. In those last seconds, in that eternity of contemplation, he decided to end it right there.

Jay once sent me a Facebook message commenting on the fact that my band got a lot of gigs. He asked how he might do the same. I gave him some advice and he thanked me. But he didn't come back and ask me how to deal with a broken heart. I would have told him to graciously accept the pain as a new part of himself—one that would always be there to some degree. I would have suggested he go on a one-man quest to better himself—every time he felt mad he should do push-ups and go jogging until he was exhausted. I would tell him that he should work harder than he ever had at his craft, that he should keep a daily journal and acknowledge his feelings, that he should get healthy and not look back. Maybe even move away and start fresh. I would have told him these things because I have felt angry and desperate, too. I have wanted to prove things about myself to people. I know it takes saintly discipline and will to stay on track when things aren't going right. But he never asked.

Sometimes I wonder if Jay was a hero. He was a fool with a gun, a dangerous fool, but he died in the snow by his own hand. He finally did something decisive that didn't end in mediocrity. Was he finally satisfied? There's an old saying that when you die alone you're a hero. Was Jay Paulson finally a wintertime hero with a broken heart and a broken head on a frozen Pittsburgh lawn? There would be no more Jay Paulson original songs about partying in the sun, but then again Jay knew nothing about being happy in summer. He was a Pittsburgh truck driver of the night: a brooder, a loner. He spent his life chasing things that didn't make him happy.

There's something I call "pushing the reset button" when you're mentally stuck, which in my younger days meant getting really drunk and then waking up the next day and trying to put the puzzle back together. Now it means something else entirely, a way to acknowledge your feelings, disengage from them, imagine where you want to be and move towards it. It's a way to defuse how you feel so you can make rational decisions. Jay needed to hit the reset button. Why couldn't he? Why does love make such stupid lonely desperadoes out of people?

The Mt. Washington Monument

Melanie Cox McCluskey

Giorgi Graziello shows up to his appointment with the real estate agent in a pristine white Escalade and a tracksuit. From the cobblestone driveway beside the home, he says he and his business partner are interested in tearing the house down and building three townhouses in their place.

Giorgi follows the realtor inside to retrieve documents detailing the zoning of the structure. Despite its location and age, the house isn't a historic landmark, so it can be torn down. Giorgi has a vision: three units side by side, each with a rooftop deck, a garage underneath, and in between, a waterfall of windows in a high-end, loft-type space.

He doesn't really care about what's inside, he says. He'll take a look around, take in the view. It's the late afternoon on a stifling hot August day, and the sun hasn't really headed toward the horizon of the Ohio River yet. It's still burning in through the house's windows. Semi-circles, buttress-topped diamonds, vast unpaned rectangles—they're all portraits on the city's glory. The agent feels the sweat clinging to her back. The stained glass, the cherry molding, the tin ceiling in the kitchen are nice, Giorgi says. Maybe his girlfriend's uncle can salvage them or something. But the real worth here is the view, he thinks. He can buy the lot, tear the structure down, invest a million to build, and then sell three units for a million each.

From downtown Pittsburgh, or any of the bridges that stretch southward into the towering wall of trees that bolster Mt. Washington, you can see the faded Victorian house. Crane your neck to the very top of the mountain, and a parade of buildings—miniature against the endless sky—looks down from the perch. I always notice the grandeur of St. Mary of the Mount Church first, its steeple glowing gold against the sky, whether it's 3 a.m. clear-headed loneliness on the Ft. Pitt Bridge, or 5 p.m. in a deafening rush hour and a blinding sunset glancing off the river and metal all around.

But three buildings west of the Catholic church is a three-story Victorian home with precious turrets, a riot of windows, and personality to spare. The quaint shades of burgundy, yellow, and black still complement each other, even though the colors have faded into sepia tones by now. Scalloped shingles on the roof, gingerbread trim, and dainty spindles keep the whole artifact from tumbling over the side of the cliff and into the Monongahela River.

When the endless sky behind the dollhouse at 520 Grandview Avenue grows moody, the vignette of mountain, horizon, and house looks faded behind a vintage Instagram filter.

Rachel is a developer from New York City. She is petite and attractive, with collagen injections in her lips and a 20-ounce cup of coffee in hand at her 6:30 p.m. appointment. She's been tearing down and building up and selling back for decades, mostly in Manhattan, and is curious about the potential of this once-loved place. She appreciates the money and the designer touches that were once poured into it, the black wrought-iron of the spiral staircase that leads from the second to third floors. She points out details to the realtor, explains why they once cost so much money.

Even as Rachel admires the faded beauty of the living space, she wants to see the basement, so the realtor and the developer head down together.

"I don't smell rats or mice down here," Rachel says, impressed. "And they smell different from each other, you know."

"I didn't know that." The realtor is incredulous. "How do you know that they smell different?"

Rachel laughs. "I've had a lot of experience."

The crumbled luxury of this house reminds Rachel of the thick tome on the history of Harlem that she read recently. Together, the two women stand in the kitchen, watching the city lights come up as the sky fades over the whole scene, from Oakland to the West End. From a vantage point that encompasses the depths of Downtown's decay and the shiny promise of North Shore redevelopment, they talk about the future of Pittsburgh.

The pink silk moiré wallpaper. The plush carpeting, once two inches thick. The electrical cords coming out of a hole in the living room carpeting are a modern-day version of the outlets in the flooring that new, expensive Pittsburgh homes have. The thick cherry woodwork at the entry way and in the dentile crown molding. The black-and-white tile on the second floor, set in diagonal stripes to create the illusion of sliding gently into the rivers below.

Roseanne and Jerry live in Mt. Washington, pretty close to the house. Roseanne says she's had her eye on this house for as long as she can remember.

Roseanne adores this house, inside and out. Jerry notices the asbestos stuffed into the fireplace in the dining room, the peeling wallpaper, the outdated appliances in the kitchen. They throw out numbers estimating how much it would cost to fix the place up. Roseanne takes a few photos as mementoes from her trip inside. She documents the wet bar detailed with stained-glass windows, the bold floral black-and-white wallpaper of the second-floor living room, the grey-veined marble mantle on the first floor. This place is like walking through a dream, she says. Her imagination goes on and on, until she is lost in a picture of what this house once was, when it was a home of rarefied elegance.

Jerry says no, never. It's just not worth it. I'm sorry, dear. Roseanne sighs. She's glad she's seen it. She treasures the fantasy, the glimpse into another world.

The houses and condos along Grandview Avenue sell for a million, easy.
From the city, it looks like Mt. Washington is a nice, rounded peak. But Grandview, like the rest of Pittsburgh, rolls up and down along the ridge of the cliff side. Turn your back on the city and head down the other side of the mountain, where the view recedes behind you, and so do the property values. The middle-class homes have that distinct aesthetic of Pittsburgh's blue-collar neighborhoods. Small front yards with a narrow concrete path separating adjacent lots, front porch, brick or aluminum siding, sometimes a third floor with a dormer window set into the roof.

Stefanie and Ray are impatient. They arrive 20 minutes early to their appointment and accuse the agent of being late when she shows up at 9:57 a.m. They are gray-haired empty nesters, bitter toward their grown children who have left so many rooms of childhood relics forgotten in their big four-bedroom home in Plum Borough.

They are high-school sweethearts who grew up in this neighborhood and graduated together from the long-gone South High School a few blocks east. Back then Mt. Washington was a working-class neighborhood. Most of the time, thick pollution from the steel mills fully obscured the view. Before it became a destination for fine dining, wedding parties and prom-goers, Mt. Washington was nothing special to outsiders.

The idea of returning to the roots of their youth tempts Stefanie and Ray.

Ray tells the story of working as a teenage lifeguard at the public pool in the South Side in 1974. At 9 a.m. every weekday summer morning, he reports to work and heads down into the supply room to prepare the pool chemicals for the day. Through the dusty window of the pool house, he can see the Cathedral of Learning as clear as a picture, he says. He heads upstairs with his bucket of chemicals and fulfills his duties. When he returns to the supply room, the pipe from the J&L Steel Mill has discharged its daily soot into the summer air. He can't see five feet beyond the window, now.

And then there's the view. The public can see a view from the overlooks near the incline stations. Some of the other restaurants offer their own spin on the heady experience of looking down onto the buzz of urban transport and twinkling lights. But from the third-floor turret of 520 Grandview Avenue, the 360-degree view scopes not only north to the city and the rivers, but also to the south and its pastoral green suburbs rising into the sky on their own mountains.

Tracetia takes a bus from Downtown and walks to her appointment at the house, smoking a cigarette, white earbuds in her ear. She wears black dollar-store slippers, a short brown fur jacket and a small gold kernel in the space between her top two front teeth.

She says she and her husband will pay cash. The realtor is annoyed, feels her time is being wasted, but takes Tracetia through the rooms of the house, half-heartedly pointing out its features. Tracetia takes out her phone and starts snapping pictures of random walls and windows. The realtor leads her up the two flights of stairs to the third floor, once the domain of the teen-age girl who lived here in the 1980s. The room is wallpapered in Boynton characters and has a small porch overlooking the corner of Grandview Avenue and PJ McArdle Roadway. A huge bathroom has a mirror running the length of the double-sink vanity. Tracetia stands behind the realtor and snaps clandestine photos of the realtor reflected in the mirror. Tracetia says she likes the blood-red Jacuzzi tub that's set into the turret with a prime view into the green turf of Heinz Field. Walking back down the shaky spiral stairs, the realtor is no longer annoyed. She feels guarded and suspicious.

When they return to the ground floor, Tracetia announces that she'd like to see the basement. The realtor grabs her phone from her purse sitting on the mantel and leads her down, turning on every light that works, as well as the flashlight on her smartphone. They venture into the depths of the basement, down a long corridor that ends in a big, empty room with stone walls. The realtor announces that she's seen enough and slides past Tracetia toward the stairwell. It's mid-morning, but the agent feels like she is being cased, and wonders exactly what this buyer's angle is, anyway. Her thoughts flash to the realtor murdered in Arkansas.

The agent hurries Tracetia outside and they stand on the front porch. The realtor is done with whatever game they are playing. Tracetia says she'd like to come back next Friday and says she'll bring her husband and their contractor.

"What's your contractor's name?" the realtor says.

Tracetia laughs.

"Oh, I don't know," she says. "I have it in my phone somewhere. I have everything in my phone."

Tracetia takes out her phone and starts taking pictures of the front door and the railings on the front porch. She's waving the phone around haphazardly and absently takes a few shots of the agent.

The agent walks off the front porch toward where her Volkswagen is parked next to the classic Camaro that belongs to the seller. She means business.

"If you want to make an offer on this house, you'll have to write a check for at least $10,000 in hand money," she tells Tracetia.

Tracetia is confused.

"No, we're going to pay cash for it," she says.

The realtor pulls out the state consumer notice that all customers are required to sign when talking about real estate.

"Well, you'll have to show proof of funds with your offer, if you're paying cash," the realtor says. "As well as the check for $10,000 in hand money."

The realtor pulls out a pen.

"And you'll have to sign this consumer notice too, which explains my role as an agent," she says, then reads through the document for Tracetia.

Tracetia signs the document, then looks around.

"Well, I'll give you a call and let you know if we want to come back next Friday morning to look again with our contractor," Tracetia says.

"OK," says the realtor. "Have a good day."

Tracetia squints and stares up Grandview Avenue.

"Well, now I got to find a bus to take me back Downtown," she says.

"I guess you could take the same one you took up here."

"I don't know when that one's running again."

"Well, good luck," the agent says. "Let me know about the contractor."

The agent turns to her car and sets her purse in the passenger seat, turns on the ignition. By the time she backs out of the cobblestone driveway, Tracetia is gone.

Rust Belt Heroin Chic

Ben Gwin

Summer 2014

At the far end of the West End meeting room, there's an old disco ball hanging above the coffee pot. The meeting that's about to start is listed as one about alcoholism, but maybe half the people in attendance are recovering heroin addicts—many of them from halfway houses and renewal programs. A few kids sit at folding tables, puffing on e-cigarettes and vapes. Little clouds of mist rise towards the ceiling fan. When I got sober in 2005, you could smoke in there. The walls are still stained nicotine-yellow.

Spring 2009

When you're involved in a custody case in Allegheny County, one of the first requirements is parenting class. The class Gracie's mom and I are assigned takes place in an East End elementary school—a gray stone building with a fenced-in playground. Before class starts, I stand in the shade with my coffee, smoking a cigarette. Across the street, kids play home run derby with a metal bat and tennis ball. It smells like last night's rain.

Inside there's a projector and a bunch of tables set up in the cafeteria. I grab a pamphlet and sit. Seats fill slowly. No one says much. Jane shows up in sweatpants, stuffing a half-smoked Newport back into her pack. She sits next to me and smiles as if I were a friend she just ran into at the supermarket. Class will run for two hours with a break in the middle.

We watch a slide show that teaches such salient points as: don't hit your child, don't hit your co-parent, don't fight in front of your child. Get your child to school every day. Feed your child every day. Bathe your child. Do not use drugs around your child.

At break, when I go outside to smoke, the shade is gone and so are the kids playing ball. Jane looks high, but I probably do, too. My eyes itch and they have dark circles beneath them. Jane pulls the half-smoked Newport from her pack and asks me for my lighter, which I hand over and stare at until she's finished lighting her cigarette. I motion for it back. She tells me she can't afford court. I tell her I don't care.

August 2009

When I start graduate school, Gracie stays with me two nights a week. I have three night classes and two dinner shifts at the restaurant. I'm living in Avalon.

My lawyer tells me calling Children's Youth Services is a last resort. Avoid confrontation, he says. Write everything down.

I make lists on envelopes and use them as bookmarks.

Fall 2009
- Jane is six hours late for agreed drop-off time.
- Jane is two hours early for agreed drop-off time.
- Jane asks for money for diapers. I bring diapers to her grandma's house. She already has diapers.
- Jane says she needs money for gas to get to her shift at Eat 'n' Park. I put gas in her car. Later, I stop by Eat 'n' Park and the manager tells me she was fired months ago. I get pie and coffee.

Summer 2014

Outside the meeting room in the lobby, there's a vending machine and a Big Buck Hunter video game. The woman behind the counter is wearing a T-shirt with wolves on it and an ankle bracelet with a blinking green light. She gives me a coffee, I drop a dollar in the tip jar and look around to see if any of my friends made it down. Past the vending machine there's a chalkboard where people write the names of recovering addicts and alcoholics who have died, details of the funeral arrangements, and upcoming NA dances.

The previous winter, fentanyl-laced heroin called "Theraflu" led to a rash of overdoses. Close to 30 people died in a week. Recovering addicts spoke in meetings about how they wanted to go out and shoot the dope that was killing everyone. Newspapers ran stories of kids dying and think-pieces on the heroin crisis. The stories mentioned the initial flood of prescription drugs, the government regulations and resulting rise in prices. Suburban kids who'd gotten hooked on grandma's cancer meds started going the North Side for $10 bags of dope rather than shell out $80 a pill for Oxycontin. In 2006, the killer heroin was called, "Get High Or Die Trying." The same thing happened then.

I ask a buddy of mine, a recovering addict, about fentanyl and heroin. "Fentanyl is a painkiller, like 20 times stronger than morphine. A lot of heroin is cut with it," he tells me. "But if the cut isn't right, you can get a bag that's mostly fentanyl. If that happens, when you shoot it, you'll probably die."

I never shot heroin. I drank. At my worst, I might blackout after three drinks or twenty. I had auditory hallucinations. I drank in the morning. I shook. I puked. I fought. I treated everyone in my life like garbage, and lost almost everything. But I played it all up as part of being a writer. I put great effort into living like some kind of Kerouac wannabe, so I could write about all the wild shit I did. Towards the end, I barely left my apartment. I barely wrote.

Oct. – Nov. 2009

- Jane moved out of her grandmother's house and into an apartment with her friend Lisa in Perrysville.
- Lisa and Jane's apartment is one-bedroom. There are two dogs. Smells like weed and piss.
- Fridge is full of crab legs and German chocolate cake.
- Stopped by Jane's apartment after work around 11; brought table scraps for the dogs. No one was there. Jane's phone went straight to voicemail.

My lawyer files an emergency motion to remove Gracie from the apartment in Perrysville. Gracie stays with me until Jane moves in with her mom, and we start sharing custody again.

December 2009

Jane is hospitalized after crashing her car at 3 a.m. Gracie was home sleeping. Her mother didn't know she had left.

Jane's mother lives in Evan's City, a small town in Butler County. Both *The Crazies* and *Night of the Living Dead* were filmed there. About a week after the car accident, I head up for Gracie's Christmas pageant. I step into the church basement, holding the puzzle I wrapped in the parking lot. Inside, I see Jane with a bag of frozen vegetables pressed against her cheek, sitting at a card table, drinking cider from a straw. I sit across from her, and she takes away the bag. One eye won't open, the other is dark red. Blue stitches cross her face like rivers.

Jane says, "I fell asleep at the wheel." She adjusts the bag. "I could have died."

I pick at the cracked tabletop under the blinking Christmas lights. There's a row of staples behind her ear, down along her jawline. I ask what happened.

"I was at a meeting," she says. "We went for coffee after."

"And you fall asleep at the wheel."

Jane sets down the bag and raises her voice. "Why are you being so mean?"

The room goes quiet. I fight the urge to go out for a smoke, instead I shuffle over to the tree and put the puzzle with the other gifts. Everyone eases back into conversations about the Steelers.

I grab a coffee and head upstairs for the pageant.

The camera on my phone won't work, so I try to commit it to memory: My two-year-old daughter with a tinfoil halo, wisps of hair in her eyes. Her voice is soft, almost hoarse. "Joseph," she says, "we've got good news."

Two pews over, Jane starts crying and says, "They grow up so fast." Her family consoles her. They all take pictures.

For the finale, the class sings "Jingle Bells."

Coffee and cookies afterwards while Santa passes out gifts.

A woman from the church gives Jane a ham.

Still wearing her halo, Gracie hovers at my knees. The rings under her eyes are as dark as mine.

"Mommy hurt her face, but she'll be better soon," she says. "Me and Gram prayed while she was at the doctor."

I pull her shoulder close to my hip.

"Daddy, I don't like Santa."

"I don't either."

"Hold me."

I lift Gracie up, she grabs my neck, and I watch her mother.

By Easter she'll be bloated and strung-out. But right now she's as thin as the branches scraping against the stained glass. Jane pulls the bag from her face, and a circle of parents step back when she shows off her scars. That sky-blue thread holding everything together.

Summer 2014

In the meeting room, I sit in the corner by the door so I can leave if anyone starts talking about Jesus. The lights are dim. Next to me there's a pile of donated clothes on a folding table. I stare at the holes in the lace of a skimpy nightgown, while someone shares about gratitude or God, or maybe triggers.

As the hour passes I hear stories. A stolen car traded for $20 worth of heroin. Gold teeth pulled out with pliers to pay for crack that turned out to be fake. Months spent in a condemned house in McKees Rocks, high on meth, torturing a dog chained up in the basement. Kicking dope in the back of a van. Copping psych meds in Shadyside when the insurance runs out.

In the opposite corner of the room, by the literature rack, there's a new girl chewing on her shirtsleeve. She fidgets in her chair and stares at the chipped tile floor. The preppy kid in the teal polo shirt sitting next to her gets up for coffee twice in 10 minutes, then leaves for the bathroom. When the meeting started, they said they came right from rehab.

February – March 2010

- Jane's mom tells me Jane failed a home drug test.
- Jane's mom kicks her out of the house.
- Jane moves back in with her grandmother.

Spring 2010

Jane's getting lazy. She doesn't even bother to smear makeup over her track marks anymore. The lies get more outrageous; she contradicts herself mid-sentence sometimes. One night she drops off Gracie, asks to use the bathroom and runs the shower for half an hour. Says she's waxing when I knock. I wait, knock again. When she doesn't answer, I open up the door and she's asleep on the toilet. Cigarette turning to ash in her fingers, steam fogging up the mirror. Leg wax like puddles of honey on the bathroom floor. Strips of pale skin on her legs. I go through her purse and find stamp bags and needles. I turn off the shower. She comes to and I confront her and she starts sobbing.

"I need help. Don't take Gracie away." Jane tries to hug me. I step back.

She has no one to take her to detox. She's too fucked up to drive. I can tell she's stuck between wanting to get indignant over me looking in her purse and the fact that she's guilty. Guilt I can't imagine. And she knows that I know she's been lying to me for years, even though she'll refer to it later as a "slip." Like, she just had that one little slip where she got high for five years after she'd been clean for seven. No big deal. One day at a time. But for the grace of God. Etcetera.

Gracie is watching Tinkerbell in the living room in her pajamas.

"Your mom has a really bad headache," I say. "I'm taking her to the doctor. You're going to stay with gram. You'll have so much fun."

"OK, Dad. Is Mom OK?"

"Yes. She just needs to go to the doctor. For her headache."

I take Gracie to her grandmother's and head to Mercy Hospital. On the way, I stop outside a house in Perrysville, and give Jane 10 bucks to cop a couple Xanax.

I drop Jane off at Mercy. On my way home, Jane calls. They don't have a bed for her. I stop at my place, hide my few valuables. I pick up Jane and she spends the night detoxing in my bedroom. I fall asleep downstairs in front of the TV.

Two days later, we go to the Soboxone clinic in Monroeville. None of the places that will take her insurance can see her without an appointment. The office is like something from a Vonnegut story. There's New Age music playing, incense burning, motivational posters on the walls. Mini-waterfalls flow over decorative rock gardens in the waiting room. The well-manicured male receptionist talks like a telemarketer and smiles too much. While Jane deals with the doctors, I take Gracie outside. We sit in the grass island between the strip mall and the office, tossing a plastic ball back and forth while the nurses take their smoke breaks by the dumpster. Then I pay for Jane's Soboxone and we leave.

Jane refuses to go to rehab, but the new custody order states I can request Jane be drug tested, and that she must live with another adult for Gracie to stay overnight. Unless I can prove Jane is causing Gracie physical harm, or is under the influence while she is in her care, I can't get custody.

Fall 2010

My second year of grad school starts, and I spend my loan overages on another retainer for my lawyer. I move to Bloomfield. I start teaching creative writing in the Allegheny County Jail. I'm assigned the women's class. My students who have children miss them dearly, but I can't sympathize the way I think I'm supposed to. Maybe two of them aren't in on drug-related charges. Their stories are all so similar. Stories like Jane's. A woman is born into poverty. Subjected to domestic abuse from parents and step-parents and partners. She finds heroin or crack or both. A way to cope, maybe. Then comes the crime in support of the habit, but she can hustle, at least for a while. It gets to be too much. Maybe, she thinks, having a child will help. She'll have a new purpose, someone to love her unconditionally, but when the son or daughter comes, it gets worse. Maybe her man leaves and her family won't have her, and there's a familiar way to cope but she can't hustle like she used to. Then maybe the state takes the kid to be brought up in the system, ready to repeat the cycle.

Sometimes during class, I wonder what I have in common with the men in my students' lives. In Jane's version of her story, I'm the bad guy. I'm the one who wouldn't take her back when I found out she was pregnant; now I'm trying to take her child. I make fun of her father going blind from MS in the hills by State College. Call her every name you can imagine. Tell her Gracie would be better off if she'd hurry up and die of an overdose. Get it over with already, so we can move on with our lives. I become self-righteous and indignant. But I hate myself for the position I've put my child in. I hate myself for hating her mother. For being too scared to take Gracie and skip town. And so many of the beautiful moments I spend with my daughter during the first four years of her life are experienced under a cloud of constant worry and self-loathing.

Spring 2011
- Jane's friend, Lisa, goes to inpatient after getting caught with stolen goods and heroin.
- I finish grad school.

• Lisa gets out of rehab, overdoses and dies.

Summer 2011

When I show up to get Gracie, she's crying on the front steps. "I don't want to go. Daddy, why are you taking me away from Mom?"

"Honey, it's our time to have fun together. Let's get ice cream."

Jane steps in. She speaks in an affected, baby talk voice. "Gracie, I don't want you to go, but your dad says you have to."

Gracie cries, "No."

Jane says, "These are the rules."

The stress is going to break me. I write and work and raise a child, while Jane collects welfare and gets high. Why can't I get high? Drink myself blind and come-to behind a bar in Western Maryland, covered in piss and dirt, left to piece together the night before using hand stamps and bruises.

Jane buckles Gracie into her car seat and closes the door. Jane and I are standing outside of the car. Pink scars twitch across the bridge of her nose.

I say, "You've been strung-out for three years, and it's my fault you don't get to see your kid more."

"We both just have today."

"You have track marks on your hands."

"You're harassing me. I'll call the police."

"Good. Call them. Please."

"Don't argue in front of my daughter."

When I get in the car to leave, Jane runs behind me so I can't back up.

At least Gracie isn't crying anymore. She's sitting in her car seat playing with her fairies. "Daddy, what's mommy doing?"

"I don't know, sweetie."

I try to pull ahead through the side yard onto the cross street. Jane runs in front me.

I get out. "You're insane."

"You're not taking my daughter." She runs up and shoves me. I put my hands above my head in surrender.

Jane screams, "Don't put your hands on me," and shoves me.

"Get out of the fucking way," I say. And I wonder what it would feel like to punch Jane square in the face. Feel her glasses break and her nose explode. Blood on my knuckles, getting stuck under my nails. I'd wind up in county jail, maybe in the writing class I used to teach. Maybe I'd talk to some MFA student about how much I miss my kid while he praises my work for its realness. *Get it all on the page. Write through the pain.* My life would be over. I'd see Gracie for two hours a month in some Lysol-smelling room in a building in Penn Hills with a social worker taking notes, while we play with worn-over toys on a bald gray carpet.

I keep my hands up.

Jane hits me in the chest. Then her 87-year-old grandfather hobbles outside. "Don't you touch her." Grandpa picks up a rake.

This is what my life has become. My drug-addled baby's mom and her rake-wielding, arthritic grandfather, attacking me on their front lawn.

Back in the car, I inch forward, like I'm going to cut through the yard. When Jane tries to get in front of me, I whip it into reverse and drive backwards out the driveway and down the street. Jane sprints after the car.

"Daddy, what's mom doing?"

"Exercising."

We get out of the development, drive a few miles. Flashing lights spin in the rear-view. I pull over. A cop comes to the window, carrying a stuffed moose.

He says my name like it's a question. Please step out of the car.

The cop opens the back door and hands Gracie the moose. She says thank you, looks curiously at the doll, then drops it on the seat next to her.

I get out of the car and explain the situation as best I can.

February 2012
- At a Rite Aid near Hampton, Jane is arrested and charged with shoplifting, possession of a controlled substance, drug paraphernalia and child endangerment.
- Jane pleads to misdemeanor possession of prescription drugs. I don't find out about the charges until the following summer.
- I enroll Gracie in Kindergarten at a magnet school in the city.

August 2012
A month before the start of the school year, Jane tells me she

signed Gracie up for another year of preschool in Shaler. She claims I never told her about kindergarten.

I have to go to court just to get my five-year-old daughter into school.

The judge rules Gracie will go to kindergarten in the city. A new custody schedule is set: a 50/50 split.

When Gracie stays with me, we go mini-golfing. We color and play cards and have tea parties. I let her draw on our apartment walls and they're still covered in seven years' worth of stars, trees and clouds of every color. She writes phrases from children's songs in her loopy block lettering. For a while, I have a modicum of normalcy and routine. Gracie is happy. Kindergarten comes easy for her.

Halloween 2012

Gracie is inside dressed as a fairy, playing with her aunt. Jane is nodding out on the front steps. I walk up the driveway. "You are fucked up."

"It's my medication."

Her eyes close and she burns her pants with a cigarette.

"Wake up. You're falling over."

November 2012

Jane checks herself into rehab.

I tell Gracie her mom went away to school for a month, and will be back soon. Jane writes Gracie heartbreaking letters that I'll probably never show anyone.

After rehab, Jane moves into a halfway house for single mothers. Fridays, I pick up Gracie from school and we drive to the group home in Carrick. "Mom has roommates now. Tell me if any of them are ever not nice to you, OK?"

"OK, Dad. Love you, Dad."

On Saturday nights, Gracie stays with her grandmother. She stays with me Sunday night through the end of the school week.

February 2013

- Jane leaves the halfway house early, and ODs in the bathroom at her mother's house. She lives. I don't find out about the overdose until almost a year later.
- Jane moves back in with her grandmother.

Everything is calm until November. When I get a Facebook message from this guy Steve, an ex of Jane's, who goes on a rant about Jane getting high and all kinds of shit I wish I didn't have to take seriously. He keeps asking to buy me lunch in Butler. I decline. I tell Jane she needs to take another drug test. For the first time, she doesn't argue about it. She pisses clean.

Summer 2014

Someone is sharing about gratitude or God or triggers. With 15 minutes left in the meeting, the kid in the teal polo shirt comes back from the bathroom and sits down next to the jittery girl he met in rehab. He leans over and kisses her on the mouth. Then he turns bluish gray and falls to the floor in the middle of the meeting. It is the only time I've seen someone overdose.

I go outside and smoke while the woman working the counter comes in and shoots the kid full of whatever that stuff is you're supposed to shoot junkies full of when they OD.

It took getting sober for heroin to affect my life.

I met Jane in 2006, outside the meeting room with the disco ball where they were trying to pump life back into that poor fucking kid. An ambulance arrives. I get out of the way.

Present Day

Technically, Jane is still not allowed to be alone with Gracie.

It took months after getting out of the halfway house, but Jane eventually got her shit together. As far as I know, she's been clean for over a year. In many ways, she's a great mother. She figured out Gracie needed glasses and got her eyes tested. I thought she just liked sitting too close to the TV.

Gracie and I still have our weekday routine. The roughest times are Sunday nights when Gracie first leaves her mom.

I put Gracie to bed and she says, "I miss mommy when I'm not with her. Is it OK if I cry? I can't stop the tears."

I hug her and I tell her of course it is.

There's nothing I can do to stop them either.

Rebecca Morgan
Paintings

Rebecca Morgan

Hunter or Hipster
2012
Graphite and Oil on Panel

Rebecca Morgan

Steelers Fan
2012
Graphite and Oil on Panel

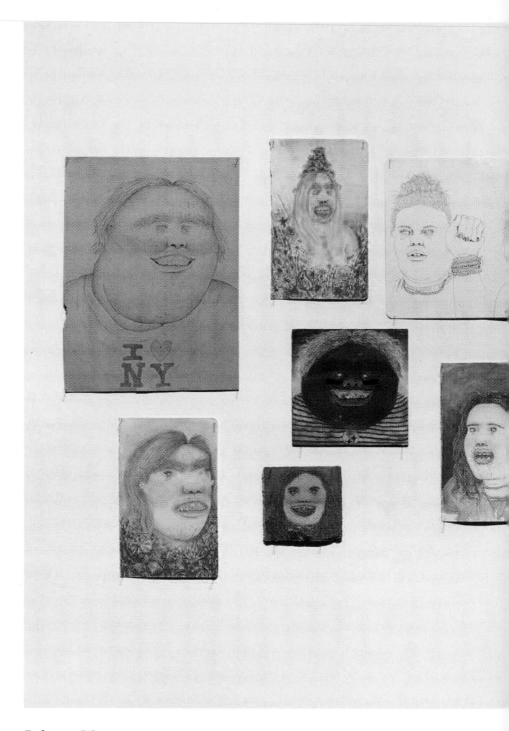

Rebecca Morgan

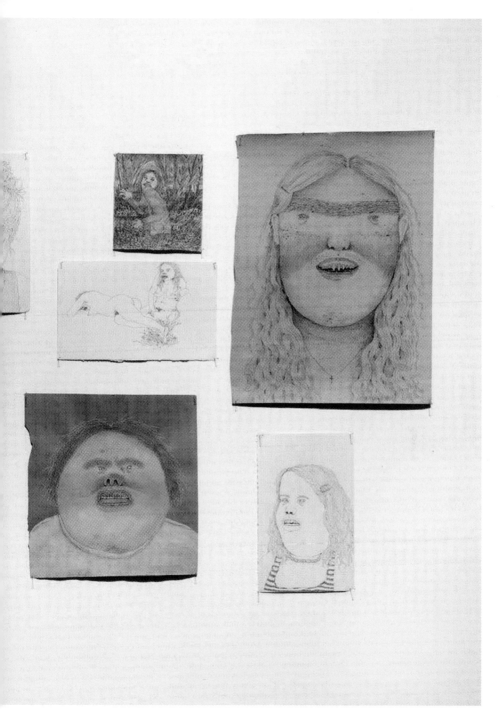

Cartoon Installation
2012

Rebecca Morgan

Keystone State Pride T-Shirt
2011
Pen and Gouache on Paper

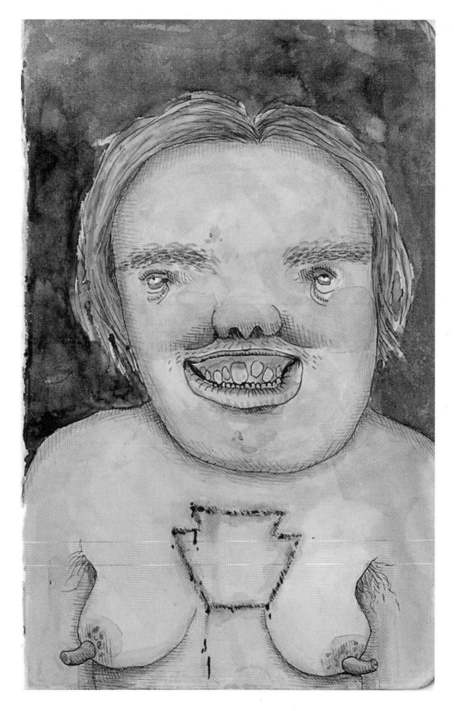

Rebecca Morgan

Keystone State Pride
2011
Pen and Gouache on Paper

Rebecca Morgan

*Self Portrait Post MFA Wearing
a Smock of my Former Employer*
2012
Graphite and Oil on Panel

Robert Qualters
Paintings

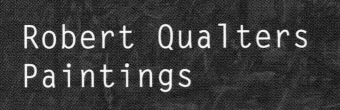

BILL, from Connelley, still waiting Unity on the hill, WAS IN HERE
BUT I WANT HIM IN ANYWAY, SO I DECIDED THAT HE WAS DIGGING FOR M

Robert Qualters

Jenkins Arcade
1982
Hand-colored screen print
22" x 30"

Robert Qualters

Hazelwood – 2nd Avenue
1984
Hand-colored lithograph
22" x 30"

Robert Qualters

East Liberty Bus Stop
1984
Oil on canvas
48" x 84"

Robert Qualters

Digging for Night Crawlers
1985
Mixed media on paper
24" x 32"

Robert Qualters

Kennywood Memories – Turning
1988
Mixed media on paper
38" x 38"

Robert Qualters

Allegheny County Jail
1995
Oil on canvas
40" x 54"

119

Robert Qualters

Smoker - Downtown
2006
Mixed media on paper
22" x 30"

Stoplight

Amy Jo Burns

A *long time ago,* I fell in love with the stoplight in the center of my hometown. Mercury is just a stop off of Route 80, a town that has one of everything so we don't feel the urge to leave. My stoplight is your typical stoplight—one that breaks during heat waves and shivers beneath the ice of harsh winters in Western Pennsylvania. I've sat beneath it countless times with the boys who loved me in my youth. I remember once a young man named Simon first told me how he felt about me as we waited beneath this light. The jeep he drove pulled to a stop next to an empty patch of asphalt where farmers sold firewood in winter and ears of corn in summer. I was just 16 and thrilled by the heat of the beating sun, the thrum of an idling engine.

He told me he cared for me, and then in the same breath he said, "I'm leaving soon."

Simon was a few years older than I was, and he had already plotted his get-away from Mercury. He planned to study engineering at a college near Erie. He'd always been one of the few everyone knew would get out of town. He was smart, ballsy, optimistic, not to mention athletic. As we sat beneath the red light, I could tell his thoughts troubled him. I watched him sit in that moment of pause—just long enough for the other lanes of traffic to clear—and consider whether it was right to honor his roots or cut them loose, a ritual I would enact a hundred times in seasons to come. Simon wasn't afraid to leave. He was afraid of leaving behind any attachments. He knew what I would come to understand in a few years' time: if you wanted to get out of Mercury, you had to leave running. Otherwise, you'd never get up enough nerve.

That was the day I discovered that when you wait in a car with the windows down, the heart will show itself. On the night before he left town, we took Simon's jeep to an off-road by the highway in search of one of Mercury's secret landmarks, a tiny bridge with no water running beneath it, a spot where football players went to "think" before big games and the girls went to chase them. It was another place for pausing, for fending off the inevitable, and it seemed like the best spot we could find to say goodbye. I didn't blame him for leaving town without looking back. I envied him instead.

My friends and I knew how to pass time together, and we also knew how to pass it alone. We all had our favorite spots for solitude—or at least the appearance of it—rusted tire swings, slick rocks next to the waterfalls, the old basketball hoop that had been turned on its side and left next to the woods. These, more than anything, bookend all memories of my youth—old, industrial things, bits of corrosion, and spaces so empty you can't help but fill them with romance.

That stoplight also reminds me of family and the town that was my family. I saw the light as much as any person in my life; it stood sentry to each of my nothing moments. My sister and I sat beneath this light, our heads moving in sync to the radio, and then later I had the same ritual with my younger brother every morning before school. My body knew the town's topography—when it rose, when it fell, and I could have driven through town with my eyes closed. The landscape had a certain melody to it, much like our trademark dialect. Nothing spoke of home more than the cadence of our sentences: *Yinz remember Bobby? The kid who never took a turn at bat during kickball in gym class? He flew off his four-whiller dahn in that old field where we used to play spin-the-bottle, n'at.* I miss that sensation, knowing a place, trusting in its rhythms so much you can abandon your own sense of sight.

That kind of trust turns familiar rhythms into stories and legends, and there are stories to be told about this light of mine. At midnight, it holds red and no longer surrenders to green. This was a tale my neighbor liked to tell me.

"I sat there for 15 minutes," he said. He'd just gotten his license and I was years away from getting mine. "And wouldn't you know a cop pulled me over. We went back to that light and it proved me right. It never turned green."

Even later, the light flashes crimson and the slow rhythm can hypnotize you like a ticking piano metronome. When I was still young with a fresh license in my pocket, this gave me such a rush. I had a Cinderella license, one that demanded I be home by midnight, and everyone I knew was rushing home to beat the clock on a Saturday night. Still, it felt as if the entire world was asleep but for me. The boys who played basketball—the town's favorite boys, no doubt—were always hurrying to get home before their coach's curfew in winter, many of them wearing wool caps stitched with black and gold yarn to keep them from catching cold. The only distractions that could slow them down were the whispers of a beautiful girl and thick patches of ice.

Take a left at this light, and it'll lead you to houses with my name scrawled on basement walls and living room couches with vials of my lipgloss still lost in the cushions. Like me, my friends lived in the same houses for most of their lives, and many were just walking distance from the courthouse at the center of town. The courthouse was the perfect spot to meet—you could see it from anywhere—and yet we never met there. We preferred secret places, our places. Those who lived outside city limits were the ones who hosted haunted hayrides and bonfires and games of spotlight. But in winter, we stayed close to home.

Take a right at the light and you'll end up in the grassy spots I used to run through on summer nights. My hometown knew how to woo its young, the grass licking our feet, so cool in the hot night. There were fireworks every July, fresh banners for the new restaurant in town that wouldn't last, and the flush of discovering that the boy you'd known all your life looked different by the glow of a campfire.

Go straight at the light, and you'll find the road I took out of town toward other highways, other cornfields, other lives. Until then, Pittsburgh was the only city I'd been in, the city that had grown the family that came before me, one where my father had restored many of the roofs of its closing mills and manufacturing plants and my grandfather had repaired many of its kilns. I couldn't find a life for myself among the silent smokestacks. I wanted to explore other towns, other stoplights that didn't know me so well. Always, Mercury and its stoplight have been a harbinger of my worst secrets. And when I got the chance, I ran away from them all.

If you pass through the light and take a few more turns, you'll drive past the house of a piano teacher I once knew. I was just a girl then, only 10 years old, and I saw my stoplight every Monday on the way to my lessons. This was a man I once loved and admired, as did the rest of the small town we lived in. He taught me about chromatic scales and staccato rhythms and how to lean into the music I played. This was also a man who liked to put his hands on his female students to the beat of the flashing metronome. Here is the secret that haunts me still: when it came time to tell the truth about what he'd done, only a few students were brave enough to talk, and I chose to stay silent.

It was 1991, and many still nursed wounds of the steel industry's demise. They'd been fed a lie about the security of their futures. People believed in what they could see—stoplights, the Steelers' defense, unemployment reports, the words of the Holy Bible. But little girls speaking out of turn? It was disruptive, troubling, not to be borne. As I watched the girls who told the truth be called liars and conspirators, I felt the need to hide in a town that was impossible to get lost in. The safest place I knew had turned dangerous, and knowing anything at all—not facts, necessarily, but truth—became a liability. I concerned myself with proper grammar and never saying "ain't" or "yinz" and learning about the virtues of Andrew Carnegie and William Penn. I performed the role of "good girl" for those around me and for myself most of all. The lie I told protected and suffocated me until I turned 18 and left.

I wasn't the only one who left town. Every young person in Mercury faced the same impossible choice: to leave home, to find a way to stay. My friends became engineers, army men, doctors, and teachers. They moved to Pittsburgh and Erie and North Carolina. Some of them moved back. Some stayed close to home, others learned the trades of our mothers and fathers. Most of us still like to work with our hands. We patch roofs and sew quilts and restore old furniture. Many of us have lost touch.

More than 15 years have passed, and I'm still homesick. The town I grew up in made me a romantic. A liar. A victim. An accomplice. It made me strong, it made me weak. My hometown was my first love for its distant waterfalls and for the countless trips to the post office and for its roads that curved like a coiled snake, and it broke my heart when so many turned their backs on the young girls who dared tell the truth. I broke my own heart again when I turned my back on them, too.

Mercury is the deepest, saddest, loveliest, strangest place I've ever been. Everyone I know feels the same pull toward it—those who have stayed, and those who have left.

"Mercury is like a whirlpool," one of my best friends says. "One you don't want to get sucked into."

The magnetism exists between our memories and the landscape itself, one full of back roads and eerie strip mines. There are blood-red trees in autumn, wind that will burn your cheeks, fires that will keep you warm and hundreds of bridges that will lead you to Pittsburgh, a place that outsiders call the "Paris of Appalachia." We have family feuds and graveyards half-full and stories that will still be told long after we're dead. There are stoplights that break their own rules: green, yellow, red, green, yellow, red, red, red, red. In the far distance there is a fair city presiding over all of us, remaking herself just the way we imagine we can, too.

Even now when I return home, I can't wait to get to my stoplight. I could sit beneath it for an entire evening, waiting for it to turn green, not caring if it does. The light stares back, red and open-mouthed, poised for either a scream or a kiss. *Which way?* I want to ask it. *Which path will fix what I've done?*

I'm not sure what the real sin is: the lying or the leaving. The question itself leads me down the spiral paths of my youth, places I've not visited in a long time but will never forget. The tree I hid behind during a midnight game of hide-and-seek, the one-lane bridge on the outskirts of town, even that black-and-white house where my old piano teacher still lives. In this way I hold my hometown close, chasing these memories, wishing some of them might have turned out differently, knowing they never could.

Look, Decrease

Eric Boyd

"T*his is just a simulation,* but you'll lay there in the bed, and we'll slide you into the tube," the technician points at the fMRI bed and motions for me to lay. But it's not a real fMRI, it's just a big, cheap-looking model of one. I lay and look up at the ceiling: fluorescent light boxes, but with these faded stickers of plants and flowers on them, as if that will make the environment more pleasant; instead, the room is filled with strange, uneven light. "So you know is just a big magnet that takes pictures of your brain, yes? Have you had an MRI before?"

I nod vaguely in no particular direction. I am too embarrassed to say I'd had one the day before, for a different study.

Over the last couple of decades, Pittsburgh has dedicated itself to technology, and nowhere is that felt greater than at UPMC, Pittsburgh's not-for-profit-but-for-profit mega-hospital. Between them and the nearby Carnegie Mellon University, the Oakland area of Pittsburgh is filled with colleges studying various fields of science with state-of-the-art equipment. UPMC, being the medical school of Pitt University, focuses on every aspect of human health, from cancer treatment to stress management. Most of these studies need human research participants. That's where I come in: I've done dozens of research studies over the years as a healthy patient. Anytime anything is studied on anyone, I can typically be part of the control group.

Here's a couple I did:

- A study on the effects of irregular sleep on veterans. For this, I spent the night in UPMC's Western Psych mental hospital, and was only allowed a half-night's (four hours) of sleep; then took a series of tests in which I had only split seconds to make decisions. If I made a wrong choice, I was shocked by a small electrode attached to my left index finger.
  Paid out: $275

- A study on opinions of health. For this I had to share my thoughts on different situations and which outcome I'd prefer; for instance, if I were crippled, and had a 50/50 chance of a full recovery through a radical procedure, would I take it, or would I take a 90/10 chance at a partial recovery that would leave me with a noticeable limp for the rest of my life? Other topics included: would I rather be depressed or unhappy? Would I rather be bored with my life or feel helpless?
  Paid out: $35, plus $10 in travel expenses.

Here's a couple I didn't do:

- A study on genetically modified cigarettes. For this I would have spent one week in a hotel, unable to leave my room, and allowed to smoke as much as two packs a day. There was a 50/50 chance that the cigarettes were normal or that they were modified to contain no nicotine whatsoever. I am not a regular smoker, so I took it up for two weeks before the study called to see if I qualified. The morning before I had to go in I took some nicotine lozenges I'd gotten from a friend. Still, there was not enough nicotine in my system.
  Would have paid out: $500. I got $5.

- A study on bipolar disorder in which I would have had to ingest a small radioactive tracer that would map my brain for the sake of a PET scan; the radiation would have been in my system for roughly three hours, total. I asked the study's principal doctor how much radiation was in the tracer; he informed me that it was equal to the amount of 25 X-rays. I was still interested, but I think maybe I asked too many questions. Plus my EKG was fucked.

Would have paid out: $800. I got $200 for doing the first two steps.

In Pittsburgh, people are pretty well-known for giving up their sweat and tears for an honest buck. Once the mills went out and science came in, I guess it was only fair to stay on that track, so a part of me is proud to say I've given up nearly every other bodily fluid imaginable. I think I even gave earwax once. No kidding.

Anyway, I'm on the fake fMRI table while this technician tells me everything I'll have to do. I grumble, "yes, I understand" every few moments and pretend to listen. The study I'm getting ready for is a joint effort between UPMC and CMU—the scan is going to be on CMU's campus in the middle of Oakland—and it's on *emotional responses in healthy people versus depressed people*. I'm not sure what any of that means, but I signed a bunch of stuff that might have explained it. All I know is they didn't have to draw blood, which is the only thing I typically ask about; I donate plasma across town, on the North Side, twice a week, and drawing blood right before one of those days puts me at a pretty big risk of blacking out. But I eat plenty of eggs and red meat, so even when that does happen, I'm fine.

We finish up discussing how to take an fMRI and, again, I choose not to say I've had maybe ten in the last two years. Why bother. Most of these studies are run by grad students who get refreshed every few months. I rarely see the same people twice. I get up from the bed and we go to where the real equipment is. I change into some Prince-purple scrubs and put my clothes into a locker; from there, I head out to a hallway, where another technician leads me to the fMRI machine.

I'm given ear-plugs, and as I'm being told how to put them in I pretty much give myself away by doing it in five seconds flat, exactly the way I've been instructed to before.

"I suppose you know what you're doing," he says with a smile.

That's good, I think. At least he doesn't care.

"Alright, now put your head in here and we'll secure it with some foam." He wedges soft, gray blocks between me and the headrest; from there he places a mask over me that makes me look like a cross between vintage Iron Man and Hannibal Lecter. Through the mask all I can see is a mirror that directs my eyes to a computer screen behind me. A palm-shaped controller is strapped to my right hand, with buttons for each finger. In my left hand I'm given a cord with a squeeze-ball on the end; I am to squeeze it in case I freak out. Suddenly I feel myself wheeled into the magnetic tube of the machine and I can see that the room is now dark. All of the doctors and technicians are in the next room, viewing me through a window. Many people are bothered by fMRIs, but I'm not. I like small spaces and, for whatever reason, the loud, grating noises of the machine are soothing to me. It's both random and predictable, a steady loop of different patterns.

Click click click. Ka-kakaka. Click click click. Vrmm, bah, vrmm, bah, bah.

The sounds are like a factory, like something's *happening*. I can only imagine Pittsburghers past sleeping to these same sorts of noises every night while the blast furnaces erupted.

Before the scan starts, a voice comes on through a loudspeaker. "Hello, for this study, you know that we're looking at how people can control their emotions; for this, we're going to have you use some images. You'll see one of two prompts on the screen for each image. One will say, 'look,' in which case you must simply view the image on the screen. The second option will prompt you to 'decrease,' in which case we ask you to think of the most positive aspects of the image on the screen. For example, you may see a startling image in which shocking things are happening, but perhaps it appears staged; in that case, you'd simply think of that instead of allowing the content of the image to upset you. Do you understand?"

I don't remember any of this being described. In fact, I'm sure it wasn't. But I've done plenty of these studies, and I know they like to throw curveballs now and then. Like for that sleep study I did, I was told that I needed to make the correct decisions during the tests I was taking, or I wouldn't be paid as much; at the end of it they explained that was just a way to stress me out and see how I could react under pressure. Not a big deal.

I actually have to stop myself from laughing because this guy sounds so Yinzer it's hard to take his medical instructions seriously. It's more like, "You'll see one'a tah prompts'n the screen." I expect him to break out into a *Pittsburgh's Goin' to the Superbowl* chant at any moment. But I say back, "Sure thing," and wait.

A few moments pass and the machine begins its scan. The usual machine-sounds and gentle vibration that comes with it. It's like a giant cradle you can't have metal around. After a minute the computer screen blinks on; it takes my eyes a second to adjust. It's just black with a small X in the middle. Then the words, "Are you ready?" appear. It counts down three, two, one: "LOOK".

A photo of a pleasant old lady comes up on the screen and stays for maybe five seconds. The screen turns black again. That wasn't so bad.

Then, "DECREASE": A photo of a woman being raped at knifepoint by a man with panty-hose over his face. The photo looks like it's from a very bad '80s slasher flick, so I think to myself that it must be. Gruesome stuff, but definitely phony.

"LOOK": a beautiful Italian market, cobble-stone streets and hams hanging from window displays.

"DECREASE": an African boy whose face is covered in flies.

"LOOK": a bored child looking off into the distance.

"LOOK": a man being car-jacked.

"DECREASE": a family having a picnic.

"LOOK": a woman being slapped across the face.

"DECREASE": a mass grave, the bodies covered in white powder.

"LOOK": a large, bloody ass that may or may not have been getting a skin graft.

It goes on like that for nearly an hour. Some of the images fake, most of them real. I tell myself that, if I see someone with a knife in their head, it's okay because they appear to be on a stretcher so they're probably going to a hospital. With others, like a man carrying the body of a bloody, dead boy, I have few good things to think of. I consider the squeeze-ball in my left hand, but this scan is worth $125. I hold on.

The idea of viewing these things for a few dollars doesn't appeal to me much, but making a living from hard things somehow seems correct in Pittsburgh. In this town you don't ask too many questions: you just do what must be done and get on with it. It's easy to fall into self-pity, and I've come close, but never for these medical studies. I was more depressed when I was a portrait photographer at a local Wal-Mart or a cashier at a Rite-Aid. I felt no satisfaction from that work, but at least, with the studies, I can tell myself I may be helping someone, somewhere. I convince myself of this, anyway.

After the images are through, the voice comes back on. "Aight, now we're just gonna do one mare struct-a-ral scan, so you just lie back n'at, okay?"

I say, "Okay," and try to rest.

Click click click. The machine rocks slightly and I feel myself ready to fall asleep. Then the screen comes back on. Is this a trick? The Warner Bros. logo plays and I see that a movie is about to come on. And no shit, it's *Willy Wonka and the Chocolate Factory*. This must be some ploy, I think. I've heard of playing movies during the last leg of an fMRI scan just so you have something to do while you're in there, but Wonka? Of all the films in the world, that one must be up there for just screwing with your emotions. It's funny, frightening, and sad. The movie plays for nearly 20 minutes and shuts off in the middle of "Cheer Up Charlie." I never even get to see Willy Wonka.

The lights come up, the bed retracts back out into the room. I get up, take my ear plugs out, and change my clothes. Nobody tells me what just happened. The first technician, the one who went over the fake fMRI with me, loads my money onto an ATM card which he says I can make one free withdrawal from at any PNC bank. He mentions nothing else so I finally say, "What was all that?"

He seems awkward. "Yes, I'm sorry. Most of that was hidden from you when you signed up for this study; we couldn't explain the types of things you'd be seeing or you'd have too much time to prepare yourself, mentally. In order to get the most visceral responses possible, we had to kinda blindside you. I'm sorry."

"Well, that I get," I said, "but what about Willy Wonka?"

His face is puzzled. He mouths the words. "Oh! The film. We usually just ask the patients if they'd like to watch something while we run the last structural scan."

I cock my eye. "Nobody asked me anything."

"Well, I'm sorry for that. It wasn't a part of the study, if that's what you're thinking."

"I'm not sure what to think, but alright. Thanks." I leave the room, the building, the campus. All of this weird stuff they do with machines and technology. I'm not sure what to make of it. Was the chocolate factory supposed to be some weird way of triggering something about childhood memories? Perhaps of the old Pittsburgh? My mind reels. The images of wounds and bodies won't go away. I'm normally a pro at this kind of thing. I don't ask questions. I just do what has to be done and get on with it.

I feel sick; then I look at my watch: a quarter till five. The plasma center closes at six and, this being my seventh visit of the month, I'll make an extra $20. There's no time to be sick now. I head out of Oakland and start walking towards downtown Pittsburgh to catch the T to the North Side.

LaToya Ruby Frazier
Photographs

Along the ancient path of the Monongahela River, Braddock, Pennsylvania, sits in the eastern region of Allegheny County, approximately nine miles outside of Pittsburgh.

A historic industrial suburb, Braddock is home to Andrew Carnegie's first steel mill, the Edgar Thomson Works, which has operated since 1875 and is the last functioning steel mill in the region.

The apparition is me.

We are not in Manet's bar at the Folies-Bergère.

On Fridays, I'd walk with Grandma Ruby to the fish market to buy black bass, and if she had money left over, we'd get lady locks and thumbprint cookies from Guenther's Bakery. Sometimes on Saturdays we'd wait for the 56B in front of Braddock News to take the PAT bus over to Eighth Avenue in Homestead, and transfer to the 55M for a two-hour bus ride out to Century III Mall in West Mifflin.

The collapse of the steel industry throughout the 1970s and '80s limited upward mobility. A majority of us would never own our homes and businesses or gain access to higher education or better jobs. For generations we inherited debts we did not owe.

Our husbands, brothers, sons and boyfriends were relegated to menial wage jobs, underemployment, or layoffs. Undermined by the mainstream economy, social isolation kept them company.

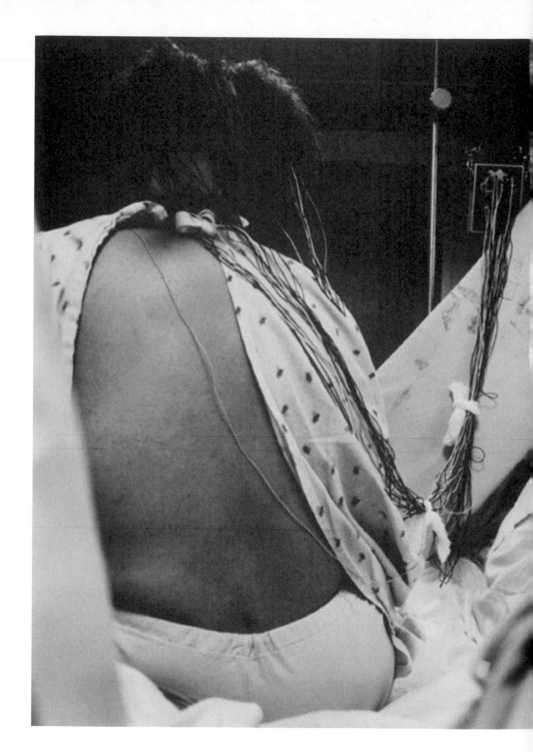

Across a hard metal counter, she laid there. Her head was propped up. Her lips were glued shut. Her skin looked thin and smooth. She looked like a porcelain doll.

While the Pittsburgh Steelers celebrated victory and Obama danced with Michelle, I clutched onto the handle with two hands. The rubber from my sneakers kept slipping on the wet snow. I clenched my teeth. In my mind I could hear her say, "You better not drop me, Toy."

I stepped up over the plot. The funeral director instructed me to slowly kneel and release the handles. My side was off. I pushed the coffin until it was straight.

Courtesy LaToya Ruby Frazier and Aperture Foundation © LaToya Ruby Frazier,
The Notion of Family (Aperture 2014)
These images may only be used in conjunction with The Notion of Family
(Aperture, 2014)

Mr. Jim Kidd 2011, Gelatin Silver Print, pg. 140. © LaToya Ruby Frazier 2015
Courtesy of LaToya Ruby Frazier 2015

The Bottoms

Matthew Newton

"We're headed down to Braddock," my uncle said. Blue Öyster Cult flooding from the car stereo. "Gonna watch the barges pass through the locks."

His white Cutlass was idling at the curb outside the schoolyard at St. James, where he stood with the driver's side door propped open and the front seat folded forward so I could climb in the back. I threw my book bag in first and slid across the maroon interior, my Catholic school uniform of blue Oxford shirt and khaki pants looking shabby against the smooth velour.

"Hey there, kid," said Bozo, my uncle's friend who was riding shotgun. "Long time no see." He flashed an awkward smile in my direction as blue cigarette smoke billowed from his nostrils; two upside-down smokestacks spitting exhaust against a face scattered with freckles and a receding hairline of dirty red curls.

It was the winter of 1986, not long after my ninth birthday. Pittsburgh looked as it always did: dejected and lost beneath a canopy of swollen gray clouds. Same as he had for much of the last year, my uncle assumed the role of de facto babysitter. The arrangement was part circumstance and part convenience. My parents both worked and my uncle, who had lost his job at Heinz the year before, was available. Since the layoff his days were often spent holed up in my grandmother's house—where he lived with his wife and son, my aunt and cousin—drinking

Miller High Life tall boys and watching *Beverly Hills Cop* on VHS.

Too young to walk the mile alone from St. James to my family's house in Princeton Park, situated high atop a hill in Wilkinsburg, the responsibility of shepherding me home each day fell to my uncle. He often walked the half-dozen blocks from my grandmother's house to my school, where he stood waiting at the edge of the playground in his olive-green military jacket—the same piece of clothing that my father and so many other men of his generation brought home after the war in Vietnam. From a distance my uncle could almost be mistaken for my father, his hands tucked in his jacket pockets, body sloped against the chain-link fence and brown hair swept across his forehead. Only difference was that my uncle, unlike my father, had a mustache that curled at the sides of his mouth.

In simpler times, my parents might have strung a house key on a shoestring around my neck and told me to walk home and lock the door until they returned from work. But after the 1977 abduction and murder of Beth Lynn Barr, a six-year-old neighborhood girl who disappeared on her way home from Johnston School—which sat a mere two blocks from our front door—an irreversible fear had crept into our lives. My parents, my mother in particular, fretted over the safety of my sister and me. To walk home unaccompanied would have been borrowing trouble, tempting the types of strangers who snatched up children and separated them from the world.

So when school let out each afternoon, my uncle watched over us—a surrogate parent pulling shiftwork until my mother or father came to pick us up. My sister, who is five years older than me, would meet us after stepping off a Port Authority bus from Oakland where she attended a Catholic high school. We then picked up my younger cousin—my uncle's son—before returning to my grandmother's house to zone out on Merrie Melodies cartoons, MTV, and bowls of Fruity Pebbles. Those long afternoons are when I first watched an odd mishmash of movies like *Back to the Future*, *The Blues Brothers*, and *To Live and Die in LA*; where I first heard "Nights in White Satin" from The Moody Blues' *Days of Future Passed* album; and where I flipped through my uncle's dusty old records just to marvel at the art on the album sleeves—soaking up the wild colors on Santana's *Abraxas* or the somber faces of The Doors on their self-titled debut.

"You know this song?" my uncle yelled from the second floor

of my grandmother's house, the sound of needle on vinyl hissing from the stereo speakers in his bedroom. "It's 'The Boss!'" With a bandana tied across his forehead, my uncle held the neck of an invisible guitar that was slung across his shoulder as the opening notes of "Born in the USA" rumbled through the floorboards. When the vocals came in, my uncle silently mouthed Springsteen's anthemic lyrics, his expression as animated as his body.

"Born down in a dead man's town/ The first kick I took was when I hit the ground/ End up like a dog that's been beat too much/ Till you spend half your life just covering up." As the song built to the chorus, my uncle bounced up and down the hall—wearing a T-shirt, shorts, and tube socks—strumming his phantom guitar and smiling as if he were playing to a sold-out crowd and had done this a thousand times before. If for no other reason, the performance could have passed for a low-budget *Saturday Night Live* sketch for his commitment to the bit. When the chorus came back around, he pointed at me as he danced down the steps and held his hand to his ear, urging us all to join in. But none of us were as electric as he was. As the song ended he flopped down on the couch in the living room, forehead beaded with sweat.

It was exactly the kind of moment that could make spending time with my uncle so exhilarating. He was almost childlike, his charisma and dry sense of humor lending a certain sense of unpredictability to our afternoons.

But when my uncle arrived at St. James that day with Bozo, the three of us were alone. My sister wasn't there and my cousin was still at school. And something about my uncle seemed different. There was wild excitement in his eyes, a strange urgency in his voice. It was almost as if I were seeing an alternate personality. And as he steered the Cutlass away from the curb at the school, he cranked the volume on the radio while mapping the route to Braddock in his head.

§

By the time we arrived in Braddock, the sky was darker than before, like someone had dimmed all the lights in the valley. From the backseat of my uncle's white Cutlass, I watched the dull flicker of the neighborhood as it passed by my window. Dead set on seeing the coal barges pass through the locks and dam along the Monongahela River, my uncle drove down Talbot Avenue with a sense of urgency, as if he were leading us to some sacred place. At the end of the street, the mill loomed before us in the distance—a mountain of blue-gray metal and smoke. My uncle talked loud to be heard over the din of the radio.

"Was there ever a time I wasn't your chauffeur?" my uncle yelled in Bozo's direction, his mouth cracked open with a smile.

"Fuck you," Bozo said. "I used to drive your ass all over this city."

"When was that? Must've been so far back I can't remember."

"Have another one, asshole. It might help your memory."

I kept quiet in the back, absorbing what I saw street after street, block after block. Between the vacant lots and buildings that had lost their shine, Braddock looked like a town that was either under construction or slated for demolition. Some of the houses were slumped sideways on their foundations, like crooked teeth in an old man's mouth. Others had porches heaped with trash bags and front yards where tattered couches and rusted bicycles were left to languish in the cold rain. Out the front window of the car the sky was almost black. My uncle, determined to reach the river before the clouds opened up, tapped his fingers in a rhythm on the steering wheel. Bozo sat shaking his head in the passenger seat, occasionally flicking cigarette ashes out the cracked window.

It was hard for me to believe that people lived in Braddock. It felt downhearted, the husk of an earlier more glorious iteration. Even as I watched black boys my same age walking in the rain, book bags on their backs, they seemed unreal. Where did they come from? Where was their school? From the backseat of the Cutlass it all felt like watching television. Except that afternoon it played out in the same blacks and whites and grays with fleeting Technicolor flashes that vanished as quickly as they appeared. On the other side of the car window every person became an apparition—the elderly man sorting empty bottles on his front porch; the old woman in a babushka fussing with her mailbox—faint holograms projected on sidewalks crumbling under foot.

But I also knew Braddock as the place where my father and uncle and aunts were raised, and the area where my grandfather worked as a blacksmith at a wire mill beneath the Rankin Bridge. That was before the houses and corner stores and bars and churches that once attracted steel workers and their families had dwindled in number. Before white flight and the collapse of Big Steel and the ubiquity of suburbanization had forever altered the landscape—turning the weed-infested sidewalks into nothing more than indicators of the town's declining health. By the 1980s, the shuttered storefronts and abandoned homes were a meager testament to that shift. Now only memory could retrieve the prosperous days, reignite the blackened neon signs and repopulate the apartment building stoops along Talbot. It was a practice my uncle had given himself to—inhabiting the past long enough to channel a striking facsimile in gestures and words, his performances often tempered by a blood alcohol level that removed all inhibition.

"This place used to be alive," my uncle said to me, pointing out the window. "Me and your dad ran all over these streets when we were kids. We'd go fishing down at the river; ride bikes until our legs were sore. We never needed anything else." He looked at me in the rearview mirror to make sure I heard what he said before his voice was swallowed again by the music. For whatever reason, he wanted me to know things used to be different. That everything used to be better.

When my uncle parked his white Cutlass in the gravel lot at the end of 11th Street, a stretch of asphalt that terminated where it met the murky waters of the Mon, he and I walked to the edge of the shore with our eyes fixed upriver for any slow-moving ships. Bozo, who flipped up the collar of his denim jacket to keep the frigid wind off his neck before lighting another cigarette, quietly lumbered at our side.

From the first time I met Bozo, he always made me uneasy. Maybe it was the yellowed mustache that spread out across his upper lip like a rash, or the fact that his blue eyes were always lost in a sea of bloodshot—with pupils blown up to the size of small black marbles. Or maybe it was because he only came around when alcohol was abundant and my uncle was too deep in the shit to know any better. To see Bozo in the passenger seat of the Cutlass, or splayed across the couch in the living room of my grandmother's house, was a signal that either trouble was mounting or that things had already gone wrong. But my uncle failed to pick up on my discomfort when Bozo was around, though when I look back I have no idea how I would have telegraphed that concern. And as a young boy, I was afraid to openly express how his friend made me feel.

At our backs stood the Edgar Thomson Steel Works, a sprawling mill built to the size of a small city, puffing fire and artificial clouds into the town's charcoal sky, the same way it had for a hundred years before I was born. No barges passed while we stood there. Instead the river was quiet. My uncle, who had been consumed by nervous energy during the car ride, turned quiet. It was as if he temporarily disconnected himself from the world. Bozo, too, seemed distant. But as raindrops quickened across the surface of the river, an overwhelming fear took hold. There were no other people in sight. I was alone in this isolated stretch of river—cold, wet and suddenly afraid.

When my uncle reminisced, he often told stories about growing up in Braddock, where he spent hours playing on Corey Avenue with his younger brother, my father. And where, years later, as teenagers, they raced cars on the long dark road out of town that mirrored the Norfolk Southern railroad tracks before opening up into the Electric Valley and beyond. That was before Vietnam, of course, and a draft where my father was claimed by the Army and my uncle sent to the Navy. Before my father became a father, and before my uncle came back haunted. What we didn't talk about while standing on that ashen shore were the crushed cans of Miller High Life that littered the floor of his car; or the smell of beer that was heavy on his breath; or the bottle of Cepacol mouthwash he kept tucked under his seat; or the frightening people, like Bozo, who sometimes kept him company when the low times outweighed the high.

My uncle was three or fours steps ahead of me when I stopped walking, Bozo still at his side. As I stared at the dark waters of the Mon lapping against the shore, I became panicked and started to sob. Not contained sobbing that you try to hold in your chest and in your throat because you are afraid what people will think. But heaving sobs, the type that take hold of the body and forcefully wring it out. At first, my uncle didn't hear me. He was too far ahead and the noise from the wind and the mill drowned everything out. But after a moment the sound was impossible to ignore. By the time he turned around, my face was streaked in tears, chest heaving up and down as I gasped for air while crying so loud that it even shook Bozo from his stupor.

"What's the matter?" my uncle asked, worried. He was down on one knee and looking me in the eye, his hands on my shoulders. I could smell alcohol on his breath, see the dark rings beneath his eyes. I couldn't bring myself to say that I was scared of him, his friend, and this place. All I knew was that I wanted to leave. I wiped my face on the sleeve of my jacket before trying again, Bozo still within eyeshot.

"I'm scared," I said. "I want to go home."

§

Two years before my uncle committed suicide—before he exited the world following an altercation on a street in Wilkinsburg in October of 1988—we stood on that shore together in Braddock, two parts of an extended family that had grown close through mutual need.

As a kid, I never knew the severity of my uncle's alcoholism. It wasn't something our family talked about. And like so many memories, certain details from my childhood are obscured, buried beneath decades of accumulated experiences. While that afternoon in Braddock is crystallized, other similar moments exist only in bits and pieces—like my recollection of a tow truck parked one day in the gravel lot behind my grandmother's house. It arrived with little fanfare, driven by a man whose face I don't remember, to drop off what was left of my uncle's demolished white Cutlass. My uncle emerged from the passenger seat of the tow truck that day, followed by Bozo. Though his car was mangled and unable to be driven, he was somehow unscathed. And that's all I remember.

Years later I learned that he wrecked the Cutlass while driving drunk, which was the last time he ever got behind the wheel. A search of Allegheny County court records showed that in late January 1986 he was charged with "Driving under the Influence of Alcohol" and "Careless Driving"— no more than a few weeks after the incident on the shore in Braddock. When I filter these experiences through memory and court documents, it leaves a challenging portrait of this man who played such an important role in my life: January 1986 was a low point for my uncle, but not the bottom.

Last time I remember seeing my uncle was in June of 1988, several weeks after my parents had relocated our family from Wilkinsburg to a small Cape Cod in Pittsburgh's eastern suburbs. He and my aunt and my cousin had come for dinner and to see our new house.

"Nice shack," my uncle said, walking slowly through the living room on his way to the kitchen. After wrapping his knuckles against the wood cabinets, an impromptu quality check, he came to the sink and turned on the tap. It was hot outside, so my uncle ran his hand under cold water before wiping it across the back of his neck. Then he bent forward and cupped his hands together and drank as if he were lapping water from a creek.

"You know, we have glasses," my mother said, smiling. My uncle laughed before walking out the kitchen door to see our backyard.

§

When I told my uncle I wanted to go home, the expression on his face fell. It was as if reality came back into focus for a split second and he suddenly remembered that I wasn't just another burnout along for the ride—but that I was a nine-year-old boy, his brother's son, his nephew. I recognized the look. It was an expression born from the type of erratic behavior that seemed to dog him so much at that time. It reminded me of when he used to hide bottles of whiskey in the basement rafters to mask the severity of his drinking, and how he would take a swig and then look at me while pretending to button his lips shut with an imaginary lock and key, as if to say, *Keep this between us.*

When my uncle pushed the key into the ignition of the Cutlass, the radio roared back to life. For a moment the interior was filled with the sound of distorted guitars and drums. But the music lasted only a few seconds before he silenced it with a twist of the volume knob—perhaps because it reminded him too much of his earlier, more jovial state. As my uncle drove away, the Mon growing smaller and smaller in his rearview mirror, we approached Braddock Avenue with the mood inside the car as quiet as it was loud on our way down. Bozo fidgeted in his seat and struggled to make small talk, choosing instead to pull another Marlboro from the soft pack in his jacket. Waiting on the red light at the corner of 11th and Braddock, my uncle caught my eyes in the rearview mirror and smiled.

The Missing Made Visible:
In the Footsteps of Teenie Harris

Yona Harvey

I *'m standing alongside a life-sized photograph* of police in riot gear. The image has obviously been enlarged, stretching body-length along the wall of an incline intimately holding 25 of Teenie Harris's civil rights images. I'm jolted standing near the police like this—maybe what the curator intended? How could I not think of Ferguson, Missouri and Sanford, Florida? The inevitable moments of unrest that bind us? Whenever I view Harris's photographs, feelings of familiarity, uncertainty, and great curiosity surface. I recognize beloved icons like Louis Armstrong, Mary Lou Williams, Martin Luther King, Jr., and many more who were hosted and supported by Pittsburgh's black residents—laboring, posing, and protesting across time. Traversing the city, I look for their footprints at every moment. I am assembling the missing pieces of my adopted home.

§

Do you have family in the Teenie Harris photographs?

I text my friend Joy, a Hill District native, mother, activist, poet, and artist.

When we meet later she says, "I don't know. I haven't seen his work. No time."

There's a familiar contradiction in her answer. We live in a proud city that claims to be "livable"—but livable for who?

§

"I'm suspicious of a city that never had race riots," I once said to Joy. We were crossing the street headed to our mothers' night out at Kelly's Bar & Lounge with its retro sign, holding its own among gentrified East Liberty eateries and hangouts.

"Pittsburgh had riots," Joy said, correcting me patiently, but sounding slightly exasperated. Joy has organized or participated in every Pittsburgh movement I can recall (and dozens I can't), including Occupy Pittsburgh, Pittsburgh for Trayvon, and What Happened to Teaira Whitehead? As a non-native Pittsburgher, I'm sensitive about putting my foot in my mouth and overlooking obvious facts, especially after living here over 13 years. I sometimes feel the disconnection between born-and-raised Pittsburghers—the descendants of all those striking faces in Teenie Harris's photographs—and Pittsburgh transplants.

§

It's 2008 and my friend Deesha and I have created a writing workshop for Winchester Thurston's third grade Teenie Harris project. Each student will select a photograph and, using the prompts we provide, write a poem about it.

A few weeks ago, third graders were just beginning their annual "Pittsburgh, Our City" project. The list from which students could choose an "achiever" to research had been sent home and our presence was lacking.

"I'm emailing the teachers with names for the list," Deesha tells me.

Among the missing were: Billy Strayhorn, Mary Lou Williams, Albert French, John Edgar Wideman and Teenie Harris. What struck me was how easily the omission of names happened. It wasn't even as if black names were stricken. Our names simply were not present. I was reminded of my initial doubts about the school.

Without Deesha's persuasive pitch, I never would have enrolled my daughter. I often drove by in judgment, suspicious of the little school on the corner, whose name, as one woman once put it, sounded as if it should only be pronounced with a British accent.

"I don't think that's the right place for my kids," I'd say, though I'd never actually visited. I'd never imagined a family like Deesha's there. We each have roots in the south, our eldest and youngest children are in the same grades, and our daughters plot sleepovers and "soul food nights" together.

The third grade teachers gladly add the additional names Deesha and I compile.

Not long after, the Teenie Harris project is born. As a creative writing instructor, I know firsthand how children benefit from the humanities and arts. But even I am surprised at the third grade students' level of engagement: they take great care selecting striking images, like the photograph of a man who appears to weigh 300 pounds or the couples leaning in dark glasses from cars.

§

"How did he live, though? How did he die?" Joy asks about her fellow Hill District–raised artist. She has the camera's eye, catching what everyone else misses—relentless, never letting anyone off the hook.

"This city has to take care of people before they die," Joy has said many times. She knows in the 1980s Harris had to sue for royalties and the return of photographs that once filled the pages of the *Pittsburgh Courier*. The photographer won his lawsuit posthumously.

§

I'm drawn to what happens when the photograph is enlarged. The past is echoed within the present. The present echoes the past. As a city transplant, I drift from place to place, person to person, assembling a makeshift family, collaging some kind of narrative. Living well here means seeing the entire city, all of its people. No matter the school, no matter the neighborhood, no matter the shine of a new storefront window, to live is to see all the city's people. It's like being inside Harris's camera, turning with the persistence of shutters clicking, pointing at this, now this, now this, now this, now this. That enlarged photograph of police in riot gear, taken by Forrest "Bud" Harris during the 1968 Pittsburgh riots, seems to perfectly capture Teenie in his environment—foregrounded on the street with his camera in hand. And on the wall it says that Harris was an artist on the ground.

I see Harris's work in people like Joy and in Deesha—it enriches the images of Pittsburgh; it makes visible what others cannot see. Like Harris, Joy and Deesha have got this city covered. They've marked footsteps here. And here. And here.

Forrest "Bud" Harris; Teenie Harris at the 1968 Pittsburgh riots, 1968; Bud Harris Photograph Collection, ca. 1950s-2007, Archives Service Center, University of Pittsburgh.

"The Missing Made Visible: In the Footsteps of Teenie Harris" by Yona Harvey originally appeared on blog.cmoa.org as part of the Teenie Harris Essay Series published by Carnegie Museum of Art, April 16, 2015.

Bright Pittsburgh Morning

Mauricio Kilwein Guevara

This must happen just after I die: At sunrise
I bend over my grandparents' empty house in Hazelwood
and pull it out of the soft cindered earth by the Mon River.
Copper tubing and electric lines hang down like hairs.
The house is the size of a matchbox. I sprinkle bits
of broken pallets, seeded grass, fingernails and tamarack
needles in the open door of the porch. I scratch a Blue Tip
and blow vowels of fire through the living room,
the tunneled hallway. Flames run up the wooden stairs.
I put my ear beside the hot kitchen window
to hear the crackling voices of cupboards and walls.
I flip the welder's mask:
Sun off the rectangular glass, a rose glint before the white torch.

The Altar Boy

Mauricio Kilwein Guevara

At the exact moment my mother's feet left the ground, the altar boy sat at the edge of his bed, in another hemisphere, masturbating for the first time. It was spring elsewhere beyond the great coke furnaces of Pittsburgh. I wish I could say there was a riot of white blossoms on a tree outside his bedroom window or the pinging of birds. There was only dark sky like the bottom of a man's work boot. Then the long muscles of his thigh tensed: oh nervous joy.

The altar boy listened for a few minutes for my grandmother's feet on the wooden stairs. They never came. She was outside in the tiny back-yard shaking out sheets and diapers already specked with soot. Bells were clanging.

My father dressed and hurried to evening Mass, holding the white gown in the air. From a distance it looked like two lovers running across the iron bridge, late for their own wedding.

N.B. "Bright Pittsburgh Morning" was originally published in POEMA (U of Arizona Press, 2009). "The Altar Boy" first appeared in Autobiography of So-and-so (New Issues Press, 2001). All work is by Maurice Kilwein Guevara.

A Middle Aged Student's Guide to Social Work

Dave Newman

John comes into the main office of the community outreach and says, "I've been in fucking jail all fucking week," then dings the bell sitting on the receptionist's desk, even though the receptionist is right there, eating a mint and doing a crossword puzzle like she always does on Fridays when she volunteers.

I'm behind a cubicle wall, on the phone with a woman who needs two months' rental assistance. She talks then sometimes stops talking to sigh or groan. The desperation in her voice makes her sound like she's stuck in an alley and the man with a gun in her face is her landlord. I listen. I acknowledge. I take notes. She calms but I'm as distant as a 911 call.

She says, "It just happened," meaning how she went broke.

I understand broke.

I understand the speed at which it happens.

John says, "Fucking jail."

He says, "All fucking week."

I'm new here. This is February. I started my field placement in October. Six months before this, I'd never heard of a field placement. Jobs people worked for experience and college credits—but not money—were called internships. I was too old for an internship. I was too old to be a student getting a master's degree in social work. In December I turned forty. I had a wife and two kids, who I loved dearly, who I seldom saw now that I was a middle-aged student with an unpaid internship and a bunch of random facts on notecards I needed to memorize for a bunch of upcoming tests. A year before this I'd taught writing full-time at a university, an always unstable job doled out in yearly contracts, until I was released with a letter that said, basically, "Nice work, no thanks." Before that I'd taught classes at another university for part-time wages and without benefits. I'd published one novel. Another novel was about to be published. For years, for decades, I'd built my life around writing and teaching. I wrote because I loved to write and I taught because I loved to teach writing and I needed to make a living and I'd assumed I could make a living from teaching, especially because I worked so hard as a writer when so many of my colleagues did not write or publish at all.

Then, like every other job in America, it was gone.

John says, "Five days in jail, not fucking good."

Phone on my ear, I lean out from behind my cubicle to make sure it's John, and it is, I knew it from his voice, part cough, part thirst, the night before and the morning after, rain and sun and snow and leaves, a desperate combination of his vices and the seasons he toughs through to make a living. I wave but he doesn't see me. He stares at something on the wall, some poster someone in the community has put up, offering services, rides to and from the doctor.

Sue, the receptionist, faces me. She looks scared. John can be intimidating, even when he hasn't been in jail. I hold up my finger: one second. I slide my chair back to my cubicle.

The woman on the phone is very sweet, despite her desperation. She needs at least one thousand dollars, two months' rent, plus she's behind on her utilities. I have the blue intake form in front of me. It still looks new sometimes, confusing, even though I've been using the form for months. When I'm busy, especially when two or three or four people all need help at the same time, the blue intake form looks like a page in the Bible, tiny rules I can never keep straight.

Last week, I forgot to get a man's zip code. There's a line on the blue intake form, an inch long, maybe shorter, and I missed it. I wrote nothing. The man talked. I listened. I wrote other things, things not zip codes, as he offered them or after I asked a question. I knew his income. I knew his religion. I knew his phone number. I knew he had kids and a church, but not where he lived, not exactly, not the zip code, just the house, just the flooded basement, just the landlord taping notes on his front door saying he was going to slap on a padlock. I told this man I would talk to my boss. I told him I would call him back, that I thought we could help.

I took the blue intake form and went to my boss.

"What's his zip?" my boss said.

My boss knows the form, taught me the form.

I said, "Shit."

I called the man back. The man said his landlord was at the door, banging. He was taping a note. He was threatening the padlock. I asked where he lived. I could hear the landlord's fist on the front door, knuckles on wood. It sounded like a hammer.

The man said, "McKees Rocks."

I said, "What's the zip down there?"

He said, "15136."

I said, "I'll call you right back."

Back in another cubicle, my boss' cubicle, I repeated the numbers off the blue intake form and my boss said, "Out of our service area."

I said, "We can't do anything?"

My boss said, "Tell him to call the United Way."

"The United Way?" I said.

This is part of the process—if you can't help someone, you refer them to another organization, another nonprofit, another charity, a church even, who may or may not be able to help them or who may refer them to another organization who may help or who may keep the referrals going until the person who needs help circles back to the original organization but days later and with even direr circumstances and less money and more people looking to collect. Or this person may just fall. It goes: shelter, homeless, dead.

My boss—kind-hearted, easy-to-work for— is used to this.

I'm not.

More people come for help than we can help. Who gets help is a confusing process, for the people who need help, for the people who help. The money is not enough—the grants, the donations, none of it. One set of numbers means assistance. Another set does not. I can seldom remember the numbers because the numbers are illogical or bogus or impractical or unnecessary or simply a figure to show government officials and voters who confuse poor with being lazy. The poor have become shadows—they're here always but only visible in the darkness under bright light and sometimes look like nightmares.

If I go to the roof, right here in Bellevue, on top of the old Allegheny General Hospital where our office is located, where they generously rent us three rooms for a dollar, where we sweat all day because we share space with the boiler room and it's always 90 degrees, even in winter, if I leave the heat and take an elevator and stand on the roof above the fifth floor, I can see McKees Rocks, right there beneath the bridge, right before the tunnels. I can see the houses and the old rusted-out mills and the machine shops where no one works anymore. I could drive there in minutes. I could run there. I could fall right over the bridge and land in the dirty water.

"Out of our service area," my boss said.

We are here, and they are there.

I want everywhere to be in our service area, even though I know that is impossible, even though I know it would be worse, that we wouldn't do anyone any good.

McKees Rocks is an old mill town, the kind of place that lost jobs when all the steel mills moved away. I knew a guy, years ago, who used to score blow in an old house near a tattoo parlor, down by the river. I think the tattoo parlor is still there. I don't know what happened to the guy who used to do blow—maybe dead, maybe quit, maybe a lawyer, maybe still at home on his mom's couch. All those people I used to do drugs with when I was a kid and young man seem like characters I know from books, from movies, all of them stuck in time. It's hard to imagine someone who snorted coke in a bathroom stall with a Budweiser bottle balanced perfectly on his head ever growing up, let alone old, but I was there too, waiting for my line.

The world forgives worse.

But then, other times, the world doesn't forgive anything at all.

§

I tell the woman on the phone I will call her back. The blue intake form is complete. I have her zip code, the wrong numbers but still. I tell her that the most we ever give for rental assistance is five hundred dollars. I give her some phone numbers to try and drum up the rest of the money. I will, later, call those places for her myself. I do not tell her she is out of our service area because I want to find a way to put her in

161

our service area. I think there are exceptionally bright people, talented people, math people, who know how to do this but they work elsewhere at organizations that are not nonprofits and they do not work for college credits or for free.

But right now, we have John, just out of jail, not happy about it.

I come from behind my cubicle and say, "Hey John, I thought that was your voice."

John slumps in a chair. There are four chairs crammed into this tiny space we jokingly call a lobby. Three fans swish the hot air around so it cures our eyes like meat.

John says, "Hey Dave," and nods like he's defeated, like jail and everything else have already won. John wears a green winter coat. He is not, inexplicably, sweating.

I look at Sue.

Sue says, "Dave, this is John. John is here to see you."

Sue is sometimes a beat off.

Six years ago, she was diagnosed with multiple sclerosis. A year later, she quit her job at a bank because she couldn't stand for long hours and started volunteering here as a receptionist two days a week. Sue walks with a cane. She has a loud laugh that makes people uncomfortable. She sometimes screws up basic tasks, transferring calls, taking messages. Everyone in the office thinks Sue is deteriorating. They think it's the MS. It may be. But I think it's us. I think we make Sue nervous and conscious of her MS and she starts thinking about her MS and her cane and the way one of her legs drags slightly and how we notice it and she forgets to think about what she's doing, transferring a phone call, taking a note. I've taken to screwing up in front of Sue, on purpose. I drop things and lose pens and ask where forms are. Some days, there is enough time to screw up on purpose and still recover. There are minutes and hours when the phone doesn't ring and people don't come in asking for free food and free bus tickets to get to work. Last week I knocked over a candy bowl and crawled around on the floor, looking for Jolly Ranchers, and Sue and I laughed all afternoon at my clumsiness.

Sue says, "John is just out of jail."

I say, "I thought I heard him say that."

John says, "It is just unfuckingbelievable."

"Jail, or that you're out?" I say, trying to make a joke.

I've joked with John before. He's a funny guy when he's not just out of jail, when he's not feeling hopeless, when he has a job and some scratch.

I can't remember when that was exactly.

John showed up at the outreach in October, right after I started, when I wore confusion like a nametag. I'd been told what the outreach did by a couple different managers at a couple different offices but it felt too scattered and disconnected. We did food and rent and utilities and gave away winter coats and children's toys at Christmas time and other things too, cheap cars for individuals slightly above the poverty level, Easter baskets and Giant Eagle gift cards for other people, people at other distances from the poverty level. Mostly I sat at a desk, waiting. I read a bunch of pamphlets, but it all felt like PR, like good publicity. I wanted to talk to people, to clients, to anyone in need so I could find out what exactly we provided.

Once I spent an hour talking to a delusional man about the U.S. Navy and what they owed him in benefits and back-pay for not allowing him to enlist 40 years ago. I thought we could provide him nothing, not medicine and not therapy, but I loaded up three bags with groceries and we walked to his car weighed down with enough food to fill his cabinets. As for the Navy, I suggested they weren't worth his time. They were impossible with back-pay, especially for people they'd already jacked around about enlisting. It would be better to get in touch with his caseworker again, that woman would know where to find him some money to help with his rent and those people would be better than anyone on a boat or dressed up like an admiral, you could trust a caseworker, and so we talked until he calmed and drove off.

Delusions are not only for the delusional.

If you expect anything, even the chance for your own dirt, you lose.

§

John stares at his hands, two pink cracked babies. He wants to talk but everything you say when you've been in jail is not what you're supposed to say. He mostly motherfucks.

I'd read two books on narrative therapy before I started back to school. Narrative therapy asks: are you telling your stories or are your stories telling you? If you're only telling the worst about yourself in the worst possible way then you need to find a way to change your story, to focus on the strengths, to find a story that includes the best parts of your life.

It's like in Hamlet: for there is nothing either good or bad, but thinking makes it so.

If you say your life is shit, it's shit.

I'm making this sound simple but I think simplicity is where to go. In the next two years I'll take class after class on therapy after therapy and each therapy will desperately detail itself into sounding different from the previous therapy by citing some statistics and some scientific tics, like conversation is the same as penicillin, like helping someone get out of bed who is too depressed to get out of bed is open-heart surgery. I believe people need to talk. I believe other people need to listen and, when necessary, talk back. People who don't have money will always need money. That's why I got into social work: to talk to people who don't have money and to help them get whatever they need.

John needed money when he came in the office back in October. His truck was out of gas, stuck on the side of the road. His tools were in his truck. Without his tools, he couldn't work. Without work, he couldn't pay the bills. The story was telling John in the worst way.

John is in his mid-fifties. He's worked construction for almost 40 years. He looks it. The damage on his face is everywhere: lines, creases, bumps, scars, moles, dark blotches, fresh cuts. His teeth are yellow from cigarettes. His fingers are yellow from cigarettes. His eyes are sometimes as red as Mars. He's skinny and muscular and walks with a limp.

"I been chasing disasters my whole life," John said.

We were in the lobby on that day too. My boss was busy, working on a grant. She asked if I wanted to try to do an intake. She gave me the clipboard and the blue form. I gave it to John. He filled it out and handed it back and started talking.

The last disaster he chased was Hurricane Katrina. He'd been working in Florida when the storm hit, so he packed up his tools and headed west. Disasters brought work and big money. In Florida, John had mostly been drinking. A couple times he'd been on landscaping crews, just to make some dough under the table. Two weeks into New Orleans, John had a grand stuffed in an old toolbox he kept locked away in his truck. A week later, it was fifteen hundred, and he was living good, eating meat and drinking whiskey.

"Not rotgut," John said. "You drink?"

"I drink," I said.

I wasn't sure if I was allowed to say I drank. The outreach was not a religious organization but they had religious ties. I tried to imagine myself as John's therapist—how much distance was necessary? How much professionalism? How many boundaries? How much honesty? I decided to go with honesty.

John said, "Whiskey?"

I said, "Mostly beer."

"A lot?"

"Sometimes."

John went back to his story. He worked for one guy in New Orleans but there were other guys, other contractors, everywhere. This other guy offered more money, a lump sum for two months work. John took the job. He started gutting old houses, pulling the copper wire. He did that for a while. He breathed in a lot of mold but didn't worry about it. The foreman moved John outside and up a ladder to the roof where he nailed shingles with a gun. Then he was inside, doing plaster. John loved to plaster. "It's my master trade," he said. All his clothes have paint and spackle on them, rips in the knees and elbows. He wears painter hats. A smudged-up rainbow is dripped across his boots.

While John worked on walls, he didn't get paid. He lived on the money he'd stashed in his toolbox. That was fine. He slowed down on the whiskey. He started eating out less. He started eating peanut butter right from the jar for dinner, sometimes dipping the knife in jelly. He expected a check for ten grand, more if there was a bonus. There were sometimes bonuses at these kinds of jobs, at these disasters. Two months went by. John didn't get paid. The contractor said one more week. Then two. John said sure. He stayed on. The contractor asked for another week. Then he upped it again. They were talking four weeks now, three months instead of two. The price went to fifteen grand. John was going to be fucking rich.

Then the contractor was gone.

The contractor was gone with the crew of guys he brought with him from Seattle and the rest of the guys, guys like John, wondered how they were going to pay the rent at their shitbird motel.

John said, "I was fucking angry."

John said, "I was going to kill that motherfucker."

John planned to drive to Seattle to rattle that contractor's head with a hammer but the more he thought about it the more he felt confused. Maybe the contractor said Portland. Maybe it was Tacoma. Everywhere up there sounded the same, green and wet and cold.

One night, drunk, John used his hammer to smash up his motel room instead. The woman running the motel called her boyfriend and her boyfriend, a huge biker, told John he would either pay for the damages or go to jail. John paid for the damages. He paid five hundred dollars, even though he could have fixed the walls for the price of spackle and some paint.

That's when the depression set in.

Those were John's words.

"That's when the depression set in," he said.

Earlier I said that John was funny, implying he wasn't always depressed, but John has always been depressed. He's always depressed, only some days it doesn't sound like depression because it's mixed with jokes and stories, sad jokes and stories, but still jokes and stories. John asks questions. If he talks too much about himself, he digs deeper and refocuses and asks about you, about your troubles. But his troubles are still there. Every conversation has a moment where he asks, "I wonder if it's even worth it?" and I ask him if he's serious, if he wants to go somewhere, to a hospital, to talk to someone, and he says, "No, I'm still hanging on pretty good." He always says, "I'm fine, just depressed."

I'd heard of the DSM, the book doctors and mental health workers use to diagnose disorders, but I hadn't bought a copy until graduate school. Depression, like so many other disorders, was still a vague idea, a thing from books and TV, from films, from people on the street, people singing to themselves with dead eyes. My grandfather had been diagnosed—by a doctor, not a book—with schizophrenia in the 1950s, and I knew he heard voices, I knew he thought he was Jesus sometimes, and Jim Plunkett, quarterback for the Oakland Raiders, other times, but I'd never read anything about it. Doctors told my grandmother and my grandmother told my dad and, years later, when my grandfather came to visit, my dad told us, his children, that our grandfather was not quite right. When John told me he was depressed, I thought: hell yeah, you're depressed, some guy just screwed you for fifteen grand.

But later, when I open the DSM for the first time, there will be John. I'll read the criteria for Major Depressive Episode, and it will be like reading John's biography.

John is depressed all day, every day.

John is not interested in anything, even TV.

He will say, "I drink whiskey, and I don't even like the taste."

He will say, "I don't even like getting drunk."

He will say, "Peanut butter don't even taste good."

He won't be eating. He will be skinny, more wiry every time he comes around. He won't be able to sleep because he's so worried about work. He'll feel too tired to look for a job. He'll feel like he's fucked up everything in his life. He'll feel like it's his fault that the guy in New Orleans drove off with all his hard-earned money.

John will say, "I'm ashamed to ask for help."

He will say, "I wonder if it's even worth it?"

"It's worth it," I will tell him.

§

That first day I talked to my boss about John, she gave me three Giant Eagle gift cards and I handed the cards over in an envelope. John bought warm food from the deli, mac-n-cheese and fried chicken, and he used one card for gas. He filled up his truck and drove back to the apartment he was sharing with four other adults, a couple middle-aged guys who chased disasters like John did and their girlfriends.

John started coming to pantry. Pantry was a food bank but we called it pantry because it sounded better than canned vegetables and ramen noodles. Pantry was always packed but I always asked John how it was going, what he was up to. Work was scarce, he said, but he'd been doing stuff for a temp agency. He said he was on a crew. I could feel how proud he was to have a job, to be pulling himself from the muck. I walked him to his car. We shook on it, on everything. A week later, he showed up in the morning, looking for emergency food. He was struggling. He was broke. He was broke even though he still held the same job on the same crew. "These fucking temp jobs," he said.

That crew was going somewhere in a pick-up truck when the driver took a bend too fast and John rolled from the truck bed and shattered his arm on the asphalt. He held up the cast. Everything from the wrist to elbow was metal. The next time we talked, it was worse. His body was rejecting the pins and screws. His arm was yellow. Then the arm stabilized. Then the doctor said John would never work again, that he was fully disabled. John said, "I worked my whole fucking life." Then John had a lawyer and was suing the temp agency.

Now he's in our office, just out of jail.

The temp agency said they would settle and promised checks but the checks haven't arrived. John is completely broke, which is broker than broker, broker than before. Last Friday, someone, a friend, sort of a friend, a guy John recognized from the neighborhood, offered to buy drinks at the bar if John would drive. John drove. The cops stopped him on the way home. They asked him to exit the car. They asked him to walk a line. They took him to jail.

John says, "That was five days ago."

I say, "That was seven days ago."

John says, "It's Friday?"

I nod.

John says, "I'm going to jump off the fucking bridge and break my neck and drown."

"Don't do that," I say.

It's the first time I've ever heard John articulate exactly how he wants to die, how he's going to do it. I look around the office and feel the dry heat blowing in and think about what I'm doing and what I'm supposed to do. Social workers have a code of ethics. Those ethics say you cannot let a person walk off and die. I ask John if he's serious. He says he doesn't know. I ask him if he wants to go to the hospital. I tell him they will help him at the hospital. There are doctors. They have beds and food and people to talk to.

John says, "I don't got insurance. I don't have a way to get to the nut hospital. They impounded my truck and I can't afford to get it out."

I say, "I can drive you," and I will but I don't know if I'm allowed to.

I don't know the outreach's policy about taking clients places. Everyone who works here is a woman and they don't like to be alone with the male clients who are generally few but loud and frustrated and angry. Last year, one guy threw a can of creamed corn through a window at the food pantry. Another guy smokes weed in the bathroom and denies it while laughing. Another guy seizes and collapses to the floor and is too big to be lifted.

John says, "I really only came in here to see if you have some clothes." He flares out his winter coat and lifts his shirt and shows off the waist of his jeans. The jeans don't have belt loops and they buckle on the side. He says, "They're women's jeans. The jail lost my clothes and this is all they had. It's like a bad joke."

"They look good on you," I say.

John smiles a little.

I think sometimes I'd like to be in charge of a charity organization so I could make all the rules then change the rules to whatever I need the rules to be. I'd run my charity organization with a bat. I'd knock on the doors of temp agencies and poverty-wage employers and universities who charge students to work jobs and call them internships and I'd show my bat and I'd say, "Honestly, what the fuck are you doing?"

I think about that then ask John what he wants, what he needs.

He says, "Jeans," and laughs.

I ask him if he needs any food. He asks if we have any peanut butter. I tell him we do. We have peanut butter but it's in a cabinet and, for some reason, we are not supposed to give it out. The peanut butter stays in the cabinet, even when people want—no, need—peanut butter.

I leave John and go to the pantry and go in the cabinet I'm not supposed to go in. The cabinet is full. All the shelves are full. I fill up three bags with groceries, lots of bread and peanut butter and jelly, and bring them back to John.

He says, "I can't carry those," and he lifts his arm, his helpless arm, like a tiny bird without wings trying to fly from his shoulder and getting stuck and falling down to his lap.

I tell John I'll take him home. I tell him to wait and I go back and ask my boss if I can take John home. She says she wouldn't but I can. I tell her I want to. I walk around to the front of the hospital and find my car. I load in the groceries and pick up John at the back door.

He says, "Thanks for this."

I say, "Not a problem."

We drive over the bridge and down below us is McKees Rocks. A famous boxer is from there. I can't remember his name. Billy Mays, the TV guy, the guy who used be in all the infomercials, the guy who pitched Oxi-Clean, the guy in a blue denim shirt with a nice beard, the guy with the great voice, grew up in the Rocks. When he died, when his heart exploded from years of cocaine abuse, it was all over the national news. Billy Mays. Pittsburgh. Heart attack. Cocaine. But not John, he never makes the national news. Construction, ripped off, broken arm, hungry, depressed. They don't loop that on CNN.

But now John has groceries and we are driving, driving and talking.

Years ago, when I was 22 or 23, I started to read Walt Whitman and I found these lines in one of his poems, "Despise riches, give alms to every one that asks." He said, "Stand up for the stupid and crazy, devote your income and labor to others." He said, "Hate tyrants, argue not concerning God." Whitman was a poet but he was also a nurse in the civil war. He said, "Have patience and indulgence toward the people." He said, "Take off your hat to nothing known or unknown or to any man or number of men." He said, "Go freely with powerful uneducated persons and with the young and with the mothers of families."

He said, "Devote your income and labor to others."

He said, "Stand up."

My brain aches sometimes from how much I want to be better, from how often I fail.

John and I drive to his apartment. The bricks of his apartment are yellow, some crumbling, some no longer present so there are open spaces and dusty concrete. I park out front but he doesn't get out. He leans on his door. He sighs. I lean on my door. He wants to talk and I want to listen. He wants to talk about bridges and jumping from them, and he does, naming bridges, naming heights, until he wants to talk about other things, better things, small things, steaks, hamburgers, French fries, New Orleans, about the food down there, fried fish, fried clams, fried shrimp, about sandwiches and cold beers. We do that until we circle back to bridges and jumping and falling and dying and how bad that would be, to die before his settlement arrives, to die before he can prove those fucking doctors wrong, before he can work again, before he can build something again, or at least paint it, something, some job, any job, some kind of work because he can still do work, he doesn't need an arm, he doesn't need a hand, he could paint a room with a brush in his teeth, and then John's like fuck bridges, and I'm like fuck bridges, and he's like fuck death, and I'm like exactly, no death, no dying, not now, and John promises me he won't kill himself, and we shake on it, we are men who love to shake, and he promises to make a sandwich, because if you're going to be alive you have to eat, you have to make a sandwich, maybe not a po' boy, maybe not shrimp, but something, you need to start somewhere, you start with food.

I carry in John's groceries. I wave hello to his roommates, all adults older than me, dressed worse than me, looking more exhausted than me, all happy to see John, all moving to the kitchen to see what John has brought, to see what's in the bag.

Outside the sun hides behind the trees, and I have kids at home, and a wife and so much homework, so much homework I do not want to do.

I start my junky car and I am starved.

Brownfields

John Lawson

One by one by one, they take
The hollow factories down. I guess
It gives the sons of sons of sons
Of workers work to do. They don't
Just blast or bash the buildings all to pieces:
The job is difficult and careful.

First, the guts come out, and then
The skin comes off, sheet-metal
From the roof and walls. The skeleton, revealed,
Gets picked apart by cranes, the massive beams
Unwelded, lifted free. The scrap is carried off
In trucks—to China, maybe—and the men
With jack-hammers and yellow bug-machines attack
Thick concrete-slab foundations, while helpers
Hose to keep the dust from swirling up
And blowing free, to coat the neighbors'
Ancient shops and streets and houses.

Methodical and slow, the workmen doze
The rubble into mountains, scrape the ground
As naked as the day those
Other men, the dead, commenced
Construction 80 years before.
Then the mountains disappear.

By summer, the now-empty fields fill up
With blowing trash that swoops
And snags on thistles; doves lie secret
In their nests amid the sprawl
Of rag-weed and of Queen Anne's lace
And startle into flight on those rare
Occasions when a person passes.

At Pegasus

Terrance Hayes

They are like those crazy women
   who tore Orpheus
      when he refused to sing,

these men grinding
   in the strobe & black lights
      of Pegasus. All shadow & sound.

"I'm just here for the music,"
   I tell the man who asks me
      to the floor. But I have held

a boy on my back before.
   Curtis & I used to leap
      barefoot into the creek; dance

among maggots & piss,
   beer bottles & tadpoles
      slippery as sperm;

we used to pull off our shirts,
   & slap music into our skin.
      He wouldn't know me now

at the edge of these lovers' gyre,
   glitter & steam, fire,
      bodies blurred sexless

by the music's spinning light.
   A young man slips his thumb
      into the mouth of an old one,

& I am not that far away.
  The whole scene raw & delicate
    as Curtis's foot gashed

on a sunken bottle shard.
  They press hip to hip,
    each breathless as a boy

carrying a friend on his back.
  The foot swelling green
    as the sewage in that creek.

We never went back.
  But I remember his weight
    better than I remember

my first kiss.
  These men know something
    I used to know.

How could I not find them
  beautiful, the way they dive & spill
    into each other,

the way the dance floor
  takes them,
    wet & holy in its mouth.

I'm Into Leather

Lori Jakiela

The sign for Chief's Café in Pittsburgh was a neon fireman's hat and hose. Someone threw a rock through the right side of the sign, but it still glowed and buzzed like an electric snake. I guessed the owner was a fire chief. I guessed this was the kind of place someone who lived for emergencies built.

I hung out at Chief's because I was 26 and trying to be a poet and beer at Chief's was cheap and I liked to drink when I had poet-emergencies over heartbreaks and line-breaks and bitchy form-poets who counted syllables by whacking pencils against their teeth.

Chief's was not a formal-poet place. Chief's was a barfly place where the bartender doled out bags of barbecue pork rinds and wore a cowboy hat that looked like it had just been punched.

One night, after a particularly bad workshop, and a nice round of pity-partying myself, I called my friend Felix and he agreed to meet me at Chief's if I promised to pay for the beer.

"As many as it takes," he said when I picked him up at his apartment in Homestead, and I said, "At least."

Felix was a poet-slash-performance artist. He performed his poems on MTV and once off-Broadway in the nude. Sometimes, when he had money, he and some friends rode around in a van that looked like they beat it with hammers.

"We bring poetry to the people," Felix said, and sounded like

175

Whitman, though the van thing was probably more like banging on a can in the subway for beer money.

Felix called himself a street poet. I was a grad assistant at a local university that gave people degrees to write poems.

"That's just fucked up," Felix said about universities and poetry.

My family agreed.

"At least you'll be able to write something on those signs you'll be holding up," my cousin Jeff said.

Jeff had a little Hitler mustache. His face was a fist I wanted to bump with a truck.

"Will Rhyme for Food," Jeff said, and made like he was putting it on a T-shirt.

I hated him. I hated my poetry professor, too, which was what this was all about.

"She says my poems lack emotion and meaning," I told Felix. I faked a British accent and pretended to peer over bifocals, even though the professor in question was from Las Vegas and said her perfect vision was a metaphor for the poet's gaze.

"One must see well to truly see," she said, like it was another thing to put on a T-shirt, this time an expensive one.

§

When I first came to graduate school, I showed up in a puffy-paint sweatshirt I bought in Key West. Like all things Key West—key chains, shot glasses, assless chaps—the sweatshirt had a picture of Hemingway on it.

I thought Hemingway would make me look literary. I thought Hemingway would help me make friends. I was new and scared but I'd read every book Hemingway published, which meant I'd read enough Hemingway to know Hemingway would hate having his head on puffy-paint sweatshirts.

Still, I figured reading Hemingway should count for something.

"Cute shirt," a Ph.D student I didn't know said.

I was going to say thank you when I realized she was being ironic.

Irony is the language of graduate school. I was just learning to tune my ears and brain to it. Years before, I'd have called Ph.D a bitch. Years later, I'll call her snarky. In this moment, I was supposed to call her a Deconstructionist while quoting French theorists whose names sounded like farts.

Ph.D pointed at my chest, then brought her finger up fast to flick my nose. I looked down at my shirt, how big it was, the rolls of blue cotton sagging around my waist and breasts, the toxic smell wafting up from Hemingway's beard.

"Just so you know," Ph.D said. "Hemingway was a racist misogynist homophobic asshole and the patriarchy is d-e-a-d DEAD."

Then she spun on her pink combat boots and stomped off, thrift-store hippie skirt wafting behind like incense.

§

I used to think I would fit in among my own people—writer people, book people—and that things would be different than they were back home with my cousin Jeff. I used to think books and reading made people kinder, gentler. I used to think books made people better, that books would make me better, but there's only so much books can do.

§

Back at Chief's, Felix and I sat at the bar, a stack of ones and some quarters in front of me. Felix rubbed his nose, then swirled a finger in his beer, the salt from his skin taking the head down to nothing.

"I mean if my poems lack meaning and emotion, what do they have?" I asked Felix, over and over, until his eyes went limp, until he started playing with his dreads. He pulled them to his nose, one after another, like he was checking to see if he smelled like smoke. Everything in Chief's smelled like smoke, down to the smeared beer glasses and fake wood paneling.

The guy next to us, who smelled like smoke and looked like a chicken cutlet, his skin breaded in sand and dirt and peanut oil, said "Poets." He said, "Fuck." He said, "I should write a book." He said, "You think you know some shit? I know some shit."

The floor beneath him was covered with the fluff and sawdust he'd picked out of his slashed red vinyl seat. Most of the seats in Chiefs were slashed and I thought maybe everybody in there had a knife but me.

"I know this one guy. He brought a bowie knife to one of those workshops once," Felix said. "Just plopped the knife down, wham, like that on the table and gave it a little twirl, like he was spinning a bottle, like he was waiting to be kissed. Nobody said anything to him after that."

"I don't think that would work for me," I said, but I thought about Ralph's Army Surplus, the collection of knives behind glass, and the retired Marine clerk who liked to talk about how he trained grunts in Vietnam by hitting them over the heads with two-by-fours.

"What you need," Felix said, "is a way to get people to stop fucking with you." Then he took off his leather jacket and handed it over.

"I've always loved the Ramones," I said and pumped my fist.

Felix said, "Fuck the Ramones. Put that on. At least wear it to that workshop. You'll look tough if you lose that secretary hair."

I ran a hand through my blonde perm and said, "Are you serious?"

About the jacket, I said, "It's too much," even though I was already putting it on, even though it felt instantly right, even though the leather was squeaky and the studs on the collar a little big and the whole thing smelled like it had been through a fire, a fire that maybe Felix set because Felix was violent and troubled in ways I refused to think about.

It would take years to realize how little I knew about Felix. His dad beat him I think. His mom wasn't around. He wanted to go on tour with Lollapalooza. He wanted to meet Nirvana. He was friends with Ani Difranco. He was diabetic. He liked cats but was allergic, so he left milk out for strays. One time, stoned at my apartment, he jacked off in the bathroom and wiped it on my roommate's monogrammed towels. I didn't invite him to our apartment after that, but one time he asked me to hold a big Ziploc bag of weed in our freezer for him. I didn't do it, even though he said if I did I could take whatever I wanted.

That's what he said. "Take whatever you want."

He said, "It doesn't matter how much you take."

When I said sorry, no, Felix stored his weed somewhere else and gave me free joints anyway and my life went along easy like that.

Taking without giving is a shitty thing to do, but I kept on. Felix's giving without taking was something else—an emptying out, maybe.

About the jacket, I said, "Thank you. Holy shit."

I caught a glimpse in the metal bar posts. I caught a glimpse in the greasy bar mirror. I squinted and turned and felt, maybe for the first time, inexplicably myself, even if I was the punchline my cousin Jeff had been hoping for all those years.

I was pushing thirty and dressed like The Fonz.

I wrote terrible poems, but I wanted to write better ones.

As a writer, I believed form followed content. As a person, I was the other way around.

"Build it and they will come," somebody told Kevin Costner in that stupid movie *Field of Dreams*.

I was building myself so the life I wanted would come. Felix was, I think, disassembling, though I was too lost in myself to notice.

"Thank you," I said again to Felix, like he'd given me a kidney.

He clicked his tongue against his teeth. He held his hand out to say stop. He looked almost vulnerable in his black T-shirt and jeans, like without his jacket he was mortal, just blood and skin.

Felix said, "It's nothing."

He said, "Beer me."

§

A few weeks after Felix gave me the jacket, I woke up with a Carlo Rossi hangover, a bad case of whiplash and a bass player named Bix in bed beside me. Bix was naked and sprawled like Jesus on the cross, arms out, feet together in a twist. I was shoved to the edge of the bed, bare mattress against my cheek. I was wearing Bix's Nirvana T-shirt. There were brown crumbs all over the sheets and in Bix's scraggly chest hair.

I had a vague memory of Bix, already drunk and stoned, slipping a tab of cartoon-Santa acid on his tongue, then making gingerbread from a box and feeding it to me with his fingers. The whiplash, I figured, was from the slam-dancing I'd done the night before, when Bix's band played at The Electric Banana and did a rocking cover of "Kung Fu Fighting."

Bix's hair was splayed over two pillows. By the time he woke up, it was well past noon, which meant he was late and going to have to explain to his live-in girlfriend where he'd been. Bix had rock-star hair. Bix loved his rock-star hair. I think Bix's rock-star hair was the only thing I liked about him, too, but stress made Bix's hair fall out in clumps.

"I have a condition," he said, in the same way an 80-year-old man might talk about his goiter. Bix creaked out of bed, tenderly rolled his hair into a Rasta cap without combing, then scooped the one remaining hunk of gingerbread out of the pan he'd stashed under the bed. Explaining to his live-in girlfriend where he'd been would be stressful, so after Bix left, I would have to vacuum up hairballs that made a ghost-town tumbleweed path from my bed to the door.

On his way out, Bix said in his swollen, phlegm-throated romantic way, "Let's hang out later."

I'd like to say this is the moment when I started to re-evaluate my life. Instead, I plugged in the vacuum cleaner and got to work. I ran the vacuum back and forth until Bix's hair jammed the motor and I smelled burning.

§

I met Bix and guys like him through my best friend, Sasha. Bix was not Sasha's fault. Sasha did not approve of my taste in men. They were simply a by-product of the world she and I inhabited, full of artists and bohemians and misfits who worked hard to be misfits.

"There are some sounds only dogs can hear," Bix said when he was philosophically stoned, a metaphor for himself and other artists too deep to be understood by the average human.

Sasha smoked Salem Slim Lights and twirled them movie-star-style between tiny red-tipped fingers. She read Tarot cards. She knew her way around liquid black eyeliner. She drank too much and wore low-rise jeans and lacy black bra-tops and she was wonderful. She was also a painter, but her boyfriend Ed headed up the band Bix was in. The band was called The Frampton Brothers, and Ed, a genetic splice of Peter Frampton and Kenny G., was the perfect front man. These days, Sasha had given up on painting and focused on designing Ed's CD covers and band posters instead.

"The woman's got skills," Ed said.

Sasha was happy to help out. Still, I worried about her beautiful paintings wrapped in garbage bags and hidden behind her couch. She and I often blew all our laundry quarters playing the Ramones on a juke-box in Jack's bar and talked about this.

"This is just for now," she said.

"You're an artist," I said. "You have to paint. You have to be true to who you are."

I was a hypocrite, of course. I never talked to my musician boy-friends about writing. I played a good groupie, leather jacket and all. I played a good writer, sidled up to the bar at Chief's, but I'd written one poem in the last three weeks. I'd written it over and over. I'd gone to nine rock shows instead. I stood in the dark and pretended to smoke and leaned in my black clothes against black painted walls and willed myself to disappear.

Semper fidelis, the old Marine at Ralph's would say, then spit.

§

Even though I wished things could be different for Sasha, I liked Ed's band. I understood why their single, "Dwarf Bowling," was a hit in Japan and Germany. This may be why I went along for the seven-hour drive to Hoboken for the band's biggest CD-release party ever.

This party marked the launch of "Bonograph: Sonny Gets His Share," a compilation album that featured hip bands covering Sonny Bono's greatest hits like "Bang Bang (My Baby Shot Me Down)" and "Pammie's on a Bummer." The whole thing was Ed's idea. It featured REM's touring guitarist Peter Holsapple, the Flat Duo Jets, and Ed's band. The project had been featured on MTV and CNN. It made *People* magazine.

"It's going to devastate," Ed said, meaning "Bonograph" was going to be huge.

And so Sasha and I loaded up her paneled station wagon with plastic cups and screw-top wine. "Finally all this will be worth it," Sasha said, and waved a Salem Slim Light around like a wand, like she was illuminating every dark corner of her life by showing the interior of this 1970s sitcom car she'd inherited from her parents and which smelled like feet and had been stolen once, but then found, abandoned somewhere in the Hill District. The thieves had taken some of Ed's amplifiers and left behind an empty can of peas.

"What kind of person eats cold peas out of a can?" Sasha wanted to know, as if this could explain everything.

§

"Pipe dreams"—my cousin Jeff's phrase for when people tried to imagine lives other than the ones they were born into.

When he'd say it, I imagined the hookah-loving caterpillar in *Alice in Wonderland* perched on the mushroom that could make Alice grow or shrink, depending.

"Who *are* you?" the caterpillar wanted to know. "Who are *you*?"

Sasha and I had pipe dreams. They were as follows: we would make it out of Pittsburgh and get cars that wouldn't break down. I'd write, she'd paint, Ed would go on playing his music, Bix would go into rehab, I'd find a nice semi-drug-free guy with hair that stayed attached to his head, and we'd all move to New York, hang out in cafes, and be happy, the end.

"Here's to better things," Sasha said, a sappy song-lyric toast.

She cracked open our gallon of Carlo Rossi. We lied down in the back of the station wagon, and drank our way to Maxwell's, a nightclub smack in the middle of Frank Sinatra's old neighborhood.

"Whatever gets you through, baby," Sinatra used to say.

§

When we got to Maxwell's, many "Bonograph" stars, including Holsapple, were inside, and rumors were static-ing through the crowd that scouts from major labels were there, too. It was probably very exciting, but Sasha and I were already drunk. Once inside the club, we commandeered two bar stools, an ashtray, and a basket of peanuts and didn't move.

At one point, a man with a ragged Beatles haircut leaned between us and said, "You two are so serious. Smile, already!"

I have always hated people who tell me to smile. It's pushy, and an order is a horrible pickup line, but this man seemed kind. Besides, he had a Polaroid camera. It's impossible to resist a Polaroid camera. So Sasha and I leaned together, both of us in our leather jackets, and played it up.

Sasha wore her biker hat. My blonde secretary hair was now cut short and slicked back. We tried to look cool, tough, pursing our red lips and mugging for the camera here in Sinatra's hometown, but we couldn't hold out. Soon we beamed and the camera snapped and there we were, full of sweet cheap wine and joy in that dark and beautiful place.

We didn't know then that the guy with the camera was famous. We'd learn later, from the bartender, that the man was Peter Buck from REM. Years later, Ed would say we're crazy, that it was probably Holsapple, but I've looked at pictures of Peter Buck and this is the man I remember.

§

What did we know?

"If the desire for the light is strong enough, the desire itself creates the light."

Simone Weil said that.

Simone Weil died at 34. She joined the French Resistance and starved herself out of compassion for soldiers who were dying of hunger. Albert Camus called her the one great spirit of his time. She was, more or less, a saint.

Sasha and I did not want to be saints. We didn't think about compassion, although it would have done us good to do so. We wanted to be artists and decent people. We wanted to be beautiful and good and wise, but we weren't anything, not yet.

We didn't know anything, not yet.

§

We didn't know I'd be the one to end up in New York. I'd be a flight attendant. It would not be glamorous. I would not become a writer in New York. It would take love and family and coming back home to Pittsburgh to do that.

We didn't know nice Peter Buck would one day be arrested for getting drunk on an airplane and throwing yogurt at flight attendants like me.

We didn't know Ed would go to work for a newspaper and be known as a music critic more than a musician.

We didn't know Sasha would never get back to painting, but would marry Ed, move to the desert and stockpile paints on the sly.

We could have guessed Bix would be a balding rehab dropout and simply disappear.

But we didn't know Felix would end up in Europe, where he was sure he could become a famous performance poet. "They take art seriously over there," he'd tell me before he left. "Their poets are fucking rock stars."

I didn't know Felix would empty all the way out then try to kill someone, a blonde woman with secretary hair who was trying to be a poet, too. I didn't know he'd use a knife. I didn't know the woman would live. I didn't know Felix would kill himself instead, overdosing on insulin.

He'd call me first, collect, and years later I wouldn't remember anything he said.

Won't You Be My Neighbor?

Rachel Mabe

I *look at the faded* and not exactly clean bed pillow David has handed me. After a moment, I decide not to think about it and lie down on my back, my head on the pillow. My feet are shoeless and sockless. He's sitting on a stool at the foot of the massage table. He puts his hands on my feet.

"Okay. It's your job to complain. Just talk about anything in your life that worries or annoys you. I'm going to dig around in your feet while you complain and you let me know if I hit a tender spot."

I hesitate. I think, *I don't have a lot of complaints* and *I don't even know this man*. It's been six weeks since I moved in. Once a grand single-family home, the red brick building is three stories high. The front porch is sort of falling apart. The house, divided into several apartments, is located in a tiny neighborhood in Pittsburgh's east end called Friendship. I once heard someone argue that Friendship isn't a real neighborhood. That some people decided they didn't want to live in Bloomfield anymore so they just made it up. But on the streets around me are very convenient garbage cans that say, "Friendship, the neighborhood." So I tend to believe them.

Before David, I met Jason. He lives above my kitchen. He doesn't have a bathroom in his apartment so he has to use the one in the hallway. I often hear him playing car racing video games when I'm pouring myself a bowl of cereal or sautéing broccoli. On that afternoon

185

in early June, he came in from a bike ride wearing exercise shorts and no shirt. Sweat dripped off his buzzed gray head onto his thin, but muscular torso. He huffed and puffed through a grimace as I held the door open for him and his bicycle.

"Are you okay?" I asked.

"No. I broke my back earlier this year," he said in softly accented English.

I wanted to say, *Why the hell are you riding a bike then?* Instead I said, "Well, that doesn't sound good."

He asked what I did and I told him I was here in Pittsburgh to write and teach at Pitt, but for the summer I was babysitting a 12 year old in the suburbs. "What do you do?" I asked.

"I read and think," he said, and then mumbled under his breath.

I didn't have time to ask for clarification because just then David walked through the front door. We were suddenly all there together in the entryway—I had so much introducing to do. This was my chance to be a good neighbor. As I started to introduce myself to David, "Hi, I'm Rachel, I just moved into apartment one," Jason huffed up the stairs. "How long have you lived in the building?" I asked.

"I moved in temporarily," (long pause) "in 1967."

"Wow! You must know everything. What do you do?"

"I'm a healer," he said, handing me a card. "I'd like to offer to do your feet for free as a way to welcome you to the building."

§

So here I find myself on a Wednesday in July lying on a massage table wondering what the hell I should complain about. And then I open my mouth and really have no trouble at all.

"Well, I've been very careful about using my air conditioning, I've only turned it on twice. Even when it's really hot out I just don't use it. I find that when I first come in from outside it's pretty hot and unbearable, but if I just sit for a minute then I get used to it and I'm fine. But I got my first electric bill in the mail last week and it was $160." I move on, "I got into a car accident recently. The damage isn't that bad, but I'm planning to sell my car at the end of the summer and I really don't want to have to deal with this. Plus! The guy admitted it was his fault, but now he's not returning his insurance company's phone calls. Plus! Luke, the kid I babysit, was with me. He was fine, but I had to tell his dad about the accident, which made me feel irresponsible even though it wasn't my fault. And frankly, it was horrible to just have to be with that kid longer. He's mean to me. We started off the summer on great terms. We had a blast together, but now even when he's nice I know it won't last. I don't know how I am going to survive another six weeks."

Throughout my complaining, David sometimes finds a tender spot and I tell him. Then he works on it by rubbing it, holding crystals over it, or making a whooshing sound and sending all the energy in his breath to it. "Does it feel better?" he asks. I'm never sure if it does or not so sometimes I say yes and he moves on, sometimes I think maybe it doesn't so I say no and he works on it more and sometimes I just lie so we can keep going.

At 71, he reminds me of an old Mr. Rogers with big white teeth and thinning white hair. He wears khakis and button down collared shirts. I can only hope he wears cardigans in the winter. His voice is really what does it though. So much so that every time I see him come through the door of our building I expect soothing piano music to come on and for him to start singing about how he's always wanted a neighbor just like me as he slips off his outdoor shoes and ties on his indoor sneakers.

§

David Speer graduated with a degree in math from the University of Charleston (West Virginia) and then taught school for three years before quitting because a teacher's salary didn't pay enough. He then went into business with a man named J. Roy from Braddock, a town destroyed by the collapse of the steel industry about 10 miles from downtown Pittsburgh. David and J. Roy bought 10 commercial properties in Braddock in the late '60s including one that they rehabbed—J. Roy ran a used car lot on the second floor and David ran a furniture store/flea market on the first floor.

In 1978, David took a therapeutic touch class taught by a friend. Intrigued, he followed that with a massage class, an ortho-bionomy class (a form of healing that uses movement and light to aid the body's process of self-correction) and a reflexology class. He loved the idea of being able to help people get rid of their pain.

J. Roy and David sold their properties in 1988 and only broke even or made a little bit of money. Up until this point David had done healing free of charge to practice. Now he became a holistic health practitioner and started charging for his services. His family also left him a nest egg, which has helped with the rent over the years.

David swears that the years of working for free was critical to his professional practice, "Most people who study reflexology don't put in the time to practice and that's why I'm the best in the country. I practiced and I studied with five different people." David sees his reflexology as unique because he includes techniques he learned from ortho-bionomy.

I alternate between gazing at the ceiling and shutting my eyes and tell Mr. Rogers about my anxiety and fear (of basically everything) while he touches my feet. He says, "Most people are afraid all the time. That's society's biggest problem. You might feel fearful, but actually you are braver than most. I thought so the moment I saw your note on the front door asking if anyone wanted to share internet. You put your phone number on there. Most people would be afraid to do that. And most people don't take me up on my offer to do reflexology for them. But you called me. You are brave and trusting. Just make sure not to be too trusting."

He's silent for a moment and lets this sink in. "Whenever you feel afraid, just identify your fear and then shove it down below your feet—between one and twelve inches—you don't want it too close to you, but you don't want it to go too far down either because there's a chakra down there. So push it down and say to yourself: I can handle it."

§

I hadn't known what to wear. I'd had massages and acupuncture, but I'd never experienced reflexology. Would he touch just my feet or also part of my legs? Would he need access to my arms? I left my apartment at 11:58 in brown ankle pants that could be rolled up a few inches if needed and a loose fitting shirt to climb the two flights of stairs to his apartment.

As I walked up the last flight it became apparent that he had taken over both apartments on the third floor, and the stairwell leading up to it. Halfway up the stairwell there were dozens of empty plastic water jugs, five umbrellas in a green plastic bin, and plants crowding the window. On the landing I saw two chairs, a table, a lamp, (not set up in a sitting area), a box fan piled on top of bags and cardboard boxes, three bottles of Water OZ Platinum: Dietary Supplement, a nutcracker. On the walls hung pictures of waterfalls.

As soon as I arrived on the landing, David came out the center door and said, "Love and blessings. Welcome to the third floor. Let me show you around." When I talk to him on the phone he always says, "Love and blessings, Rachel. This is David from upstairs." And sometimes he varies it by adding an "on the third floor." The door to the right was closed and he said that he used that room for storage. He led me back through the door he'd just come out of and showed me his main living space.

We entered a bright rectangular room with slanted ceilings. To the left was a queen bed with a blue fuzzy blanket on top that had a dolphin on it. When he saw me looking he said, "I sleep with the dolphins." He showed me two kitchens and two bathrooms. One kitchen in the bigger apartment and one in the room he originally rented in 1967, which he now uses as an office. One bathroom in the bigger apartment and one in the hall.

He then took me through a door on which hung a big yellow smiley face into his office. The room was small and cramped, the ceilings and walls cracked and bulging—the room in much worse condition than my apartment. There was a massage table, an old reclining chair, a small desk, a printer station he offered to let me use if I was ever in a bind. He pointed out the window toward the hospital where he was born that I'd be able to see if the leaves were bare. He showed me his shrine on the mantel of the non-functioning fireplace. The frameless pictures curling down on the sides. He explained the reflexology poster on the wall that maps out the points on the feet and hands and where they coordinate on the body.

§

After I am done complaining about Luke, I start complaining about my complicated love life. I tell him about Davidrichardmurphy, "We broke up in January, but we still talk all the time. We're basically together, but not. He's coming to visit in a couple of weeks."

When I finally seem to run out of steam, David says, "Women are smarter than men. Men are actually quite stupid. But don't punish

189

us for it! Help us. Trick us. Women are more connected to the moon and men think selfishly while women intuitively make decisions based on getting results that are not only best for them, but also for the other people involved. Your menstrual cycle is a sacred thing. I suggest you track your 28-day moon cycle and see how you feel in relation to what the moon is doing. One thing to think about is the difference between attachment and love. Love has no fear." He paused to ask me about a spot in between my big toe and the one next to it. "Really though," he continued, "men are stupid and you need to help us. One thing you can try this summer is to practice tricking men, really just doing what's best for us, on the kid you're babysitting. If you can perfect it on him, you can do it on all of us!"

And then as if he can't help it, he starts telling me about conspiracies. "9/11 was a conspiracy. Did you know that? I have a report around here somewhere if you want to see it that shows that the twin towers fell as a result of demolition. There was no way that the plane crash could have caused them to fall so quickly. And did you know that the United States government funds UFO research by selling drugs to our children?"

When I get up from the table, four hours have passed. "Most people need two to six hours of work to reset themselves. For future reference, for you or your friends, I charge a dollar a minute."

I thank him profusely. "If you won't take any money will you let me make you dinner one night to thank you for taking the time to do this?"

"Sure. I'll look at my schedule and give you a call soon. I want you to know that if you are ever afraid you can call me and we can talk through your fear."

He gives me a knowing look and says, "You'll learn to come visit the man on the third floor."

Love and blessings.

Equity

Michael Gerhard Martin

My clock radio blared at six in the morning, and I hauled myself up. I was sore all over. We had worked seven to seven the previous day, loading washers and dryers and refrigerators into the trailer of a semi. Today we would do the rest of the appliances and the TVs and stereos. I had been unemployed for about seven months before I got the job as a salesman at an appliance and electronics store. Unlike their competitors, they didn't do credit checks on prospective employees. Mine was shot.

I'd been working there for less than six months when we got the news we'd been sold to an equity company. Inventory dwindled, and advertising stopped. In another two months the company was gutted, and we were threatened by our old bosses: show up to pack the trucks and you'll get paid for your last two weeks. Don't show up, and good luck getting anything out of us.

So we showed up. We all definitely needed the money. Alex was living out of his car, crashing in one place or another. He'd dropped out of his biology program at Pitt when his stepmother kicked him out of the house so she could host Polish footballers for the summer. There was a kid with a lazy eye who was always trying to steal commissions, before there was no advertising, and then no merchandise, and then no commissions. He was a dick, but he had a little girl, who also had a lazy eye. There was another kid who had rich parents; he'd been three-fourths of the way through chiropractor school before he lost the tips of three fingers in an accident, and now he was trying to figure out what the fuck to do. There was a good looking, dumb-as shit-blond kid with a gorgeous girlfriend he loved and a baby he couldn't afford. Kevin, our manager, was as kind as he was baggy-pantsed and goofy-looking. He'd just had his second kid, and he let Alex use his shower and sleep on his couch once in a while. Tony, the assistant manager, was in his thirties and looked good in a suit. He made good-natured fun of us white boys and wrote three separate child support checks every month.

I didn't shower, but I bolted a can of Coke and smoked a cigarette while I took a shit. I drank another coke and smoked three or four more while I drove my red VW Golf from stoplight to stoplight down Route 51, out past Century III Mall.

Kevin and I were the only ones on time, and for a while we were worried the others wouldn't show. The company had hauled off the first semi, and we had another one to pack. But the others showed up, one after another until nine, when we were at full strength. With no commission I was supposedly getting minimum wage; those two early-morning hours paid me about $14, before taxes, provided we got paid.

We started out doing it right, keeping inventory and carefully packing everything that was out-of-box. We had lunch from McDonald's, and only stopped to suck on cigarettes out by the semi-trailer. By the end we were goofy. Shit was walking off—I didn't steal anything, and could have kicked myself later, but I knew guys were stashing merchandise in their trunks all day.

By five, we were punchy. We took our anger and fear out on the merchandise that belonged to this foreign-owned nest of pricks who bought companies in order to destroy them. When a guy like that ran for president a couple of years ago, I enjoyed his humiliating defeat the way sports fans enjoy watching the rival team fall apart in the clinch. When I heard his wife cried and cried because he lost, I thought it was the funniest thing I'd ever heard.

The kid who had wanted to be a chiropractor kicked in the sides of appliances, and threw $500 A/V receivers overhand into the truck. The blond kid cheered every time a TV accidentally fell off the back of the semi, and we half-assed swept up the glass. We used the truck's hydraulic lift gate to mangle and crush. Carrying a Macintosh computer I'd been saving for the whole time I'd worked there, I pretended to pitch forward. When it hit the concrete floor with a crunch, I didn't feel satisfied. When Alex sent it hurtling into the truck, I felt sick and sad.

At seven we quit—I don't know what happened to whatever else was there. We weren't getting paid to come back again, so fuck it. Someone suggested we go to a topless bar for a quick beer to cheer the fuck up, so we did.

Out in some dingy backwater of the South Hills, we parked our old cars in the lot of a dirty foot joint with two dollar Iron City beers and three dancers in thongs and pasties. If you only like plastic dolls, I guess they were dogs, but if you like women, they were beautiful—I remember one was tall and angular, flirty and funny—another was quiet and dark and finely muscled.

The tall boisterous woman asked us about ourselves and wished us well, and we tipped as much as we could with the singles we got back with our beers. None of us had the money to stay for a third drink, but none of us had a reason to wake up the next morning, either. We didn't want to leave each other. None of us wanted to be alone. I think I was the last to leave. I lived by myself. The quiet girl sat on the stage near my table and tried to make conversation. The bar was a tomb. I wanted to ask her out but I was flat broke.

I got home to my empty house and smoked a joint and the rest of my cigarettes. I'd been in love earlier that year, with a woman 10 years older than me, and it hadn't gone my way. I went to bed, slipping naked between the sheets in much the same way I was slipping into one of the worst depressions of my life.

When I woke up the next morning, I didn't have my wallet. I cleaned the McDonald's wrappers and Coke cans and cigarette packs out of my car, reached way under the seats, got a flashlight. I found four roaches, two mangled-but-salvageable packs of smokes and two dollars worth of sticky change.

I had 60 bucks in my wallet—my last 60 bucks. I also had my license, and I didn't have $25 for a new one. I didn't have any credit cards because they were all maxed out.

I waited all day. It was a feeling like just before you're punched in the face, a taste like electricity, iron and blood at the bridge of my nose. At five, I tried calling the bar. At six, I got the bartender on the line.

I have never felt more stupid than in the moment I described my wallet, and the 60 bucks inside, to the bartender at a dirty foot joint in a poor-as-shit, brake-dust-and-diesel-smoke neighborhood south of

Pittsburgh.

"Yeah, we fahn it," he said. "Sixy bucks's still air. C'mon dahn and get it 'fore it wawks off."

So I drove my little red VW, with the caved-in rear fender, to the strip joint halfway to Uniontown. I had to gun it through one of the most ridiculously complicated intersections I've ever seen and I almost got clipped by a truck. I was freaking out. My last 60 bucks.

I parked next to the dumpster and heard the oily creek back behind a thick hedge of brambles and weeds. A big cement truck rumbled and clanked through the intersection. The place was an old house, too close to the road now to live in, painted gray to match the Pittsburgh sky. It had once even been pretty, a sharp-peaked Victorian built overlooking a creek in the sunny part of a hollow. Now it had a flat rubber shed roof that wrapped around the building where the porches had been. There were no windows.

I opened the door and ducked inside. Except for the little linoleum-topped stage, it could have been any dive in the city. A couple of unhealthy-looking specimens were chewing ice cubes, fingernails, or the little red straws that come in the mixed drinks. It smelled like the creek had flooded years ago, like cigarettes and cigars and stale beer, scents as layered as rock strata along a highway cut. The bartender asked me to describe my wallet, and there it was, sixty bucks, license, AAA card, all of it.

I thanked him, and told him I'd just been laid off. "Tough luck, buddy," he said, "'at sucks." He was wearing a black restaurant uniform vest, and when he did make eye contact, he looked startled and a little crazy.

I took out 10 bucks. I couldn't afford it, but I'd almost lost much more. I handed it to him. "Give this to whoever found it, ok?"

"Y'inz don' haffa do 'at," he said.

"I wanna," I said. I turned, waving, and walked out before he gave me a second chance.

Picksburgh Sampler—Furill

Ann Curran

Listen up, yinz. Wanna go aht
for a chipped ham sammitch 'n' Ahrn?

Ain't no place in the Burgh to buy one.
Not dahntahn. Not E'Sliberty.

How 'bout Gynt Iggle, you jag off
You can get some jumbo there, too.

We gotta make our own sammitches?
It's 'bout time to wach a Stillers.

You ain't wearing the right keller.
Was gold. Worshed it with a red shirt.

Is your babushka gal coming?
Nah, she went dahntahn on bidness,

crossed the Mon, hit a telepole
and landed in a jaggerbush.

Face is a dish of Heinz kitch-ip
Told her that and hurt her fillings.

I'm ascared to text her n'at.
I went dahnnair for pisgetti.

She stayed in the baffroom all night,
skwillin and bawwin her head off.

Kenya come back for some breffis,
her Mom said. She's such a sperled girl.

The Pittsburgh Poem Is
After Iggy McGovern's *The Irish Poem Is*

Ann Curran

a Terrible Towel, a political row, a Cyril Wecht trial
a Steeler nation, an education, a million patients
a Golden Triangle, a neighborhood wrangle, a weeping Angle
a river ride, an ebb tide, an also died
a Catholic church, a pre-flight search, an Aviary perch
a wobbly incline, a coal mine, an ALCOA/BAYER sign
a Fort Duquesne, an Old Main, a touch of Cain
a steel mill, a steep hill, a last will
a Warhol wig, a jazz gig, a river dig
a fair deal, a down-at-the-heel, a Ferris wheel
a Pirate team, a boater's dream, an Isaly's ice cream
a bit smutty, an instant buddy, Silly Putty
a PAT bus, a creative cuss, a medical truss
a maiden aunt, a red-hot rant, a heart transplant
a pizza pie, a white lie, a regular guy
a laundromat, an old hat, a bloody baseball bat
a small town, a prom gown, a Mr. Yuk frown
a Neighborhood of Make-Believe, neighborhoods that make you grieve
a card game, an Auntie Mame, a same-same
a boiled pirogi, a hand-rolled stogie, a miraculous bogie
a Mellon bubble, a share of rubble, a teacher in trouble
a Sid the Kid, a Sophie Masloff bid, once hell without a lid
a jail trail, a rusty rail, a deer-hunter male
a clean-air deception, a lack of perception, an immaculate reception
a Dairy Queen, a too-often Seen, a dead teen
a Cathedral of Learning, a minimum-wage earning, a Hill burning

a Kaufmann's clock, a violent jock, a town in hock
a Bettis bash, a Hines Ward dash, some Rooney cash
a reserved-parking chair, Top-Doc care, a baby mayor
a cool I.C. Light, a bingo night, a brownfield site
a polio shot, a melting pot, a killer caught
a coal barge, a Macy's charge, an XXtra large
a Mario Lemieux, an Irish stew, an empty church pew
a Heinz pickle pin, a seedy has-been, any soccer win
a mini-subway, a traffic delay, a secret gay
a Grandview lark, an Eat N Park, a no-longer dark
a labor fight, a fireworks night, a Romero fright
a Giant Eagle, a bit illegal, a backside wiggle

a billion stairs, a street fair, an occasional bear
a herd of deer, an old-fashioned cheer, a come-hither leer
a friendly face, The Circular Staircase, a question of race
a homeless man, a Penguin fan, a smoking ban
a bluegrass band, a legal demand, a threat to expand
a Smiley Face □ , a public TV place, a Civic Arena erased
a big Mac, a certain knack, a 9/11 attack
a lot of big hips, a bit of lip, a blooming Phipps
a Perry Como, an Anglican homo, a park to roam, oh!
a Bach Choir, a swinging tire, a campus wired
a Kelly dance school, a Hillman jewel, a closed swimming pool
a Red Door, a Teutonia Mannerchor, a Liberty Avenue whore
a taste more sweet than tart, a town with heart, a first modern art museum
a senior center, a Do Not Enter, a robot inventor
a Gladys Schmitt, a candle lit, a double hit
a local bar, a battered car, a bridge too far
a Kennywood, a creepy hood, a should-have-stood
a first in nation radio station, movie theater, gas station
a Jonny Gammage, more collateral damage, a Jordan Miles
a dinosaur city, afraid of a ditty, ah, there's the pity
a parking fine, a bottle of wine, a final rhyme

A version of this poem appeared in the *Pittsburgh Post-Gazette*

Lost City

Lisa Toboz

Often *Pittsburgh is visually represented* through its bridges, and stunning view of the three rivers from its Mt. Washington vantage point. In Lost City, I explore mostly residential neighborhoods with old Polaroid cameras, uncovering its hidden gems on instant film. Over hills, and through woods, or in the middle of urban development, it's comforting to know that some things remain the same.

East Liberty – Anthon's Restaurant and Bakery on Penn Avenue, in the center of East Liberty's former business district, is now a few blocks down from the newly developed Bakery Square and Target. One friend noted, "It always looks closed, even when it's open."

Strip District – A cold, rainy day under the 31st Street Bridge.

Polish Hill – From the top of Brereton Street, Thanksgiving Day – this traditionally Eastern European neighborhood is tucked away into the hills, overlooking the Strip District and the Allegheny River.

Troy Hill – It's always 9:05 at this former auto service shop on Troy Hill Road.

Allegheny West – The Modern Café, an Art Deco beacon near the CCAC campus.

Troy Hill – A view of the Heinz Factory from a parking lot overlooking Route 28. Built in 1890, the factory has turned a portion of its space into lofts, and the majority of its ketchup is produced in Ohio.

Rebirth of the Hollywood Lanes

Kevin Tasker

For a long time, many people felt that Dormont was doomed. Jobs were moving way east and most major industry vanished post- 9/11. One fated day in 2014, a stalwart neighborhood grocer's, The People's Food Market, erupted in a three-alarm fire, the apparent result of a lightning strike. The wrecked community begged for an outlet for their grief, and a means by which to lift their spirits. No one yet knew that a response to these pleas waited just below street level in an abandoned bowling alley, but it was only a matter of time.

Turns out the man to save the bowling alley—and enliven the community it represented—'twas a native Pittsburgh fellow by the name of Jeff Clemont. Skinny, bearded and perpetually grinning in a brown suit coat and unknotted tie, Jeff looks playfully dangerous, like Dean Moriarty had he grown up in the Rust Belt.

For Jeff, the urge to resurrect the bowling alley that would come to be known as the Hollywood Lanes (an homage to Jeff's grandfather whose nickname at the steel mill was 'Hollywood' due to his slicked Elvis-esque hairdo) began as a deeply personal one.

"I grew up in Mt. Washington, overlooking the city," Jeff says, "We moved to Maryland when I was three or four, but we came back literally 450 times, and every time we visited that bowling alley. [The place] is in my DNA."

Jeff began renovating about a year ago, using his own money. It's been a massive undertaking bringing the Lanes back from the dead, re-quiring thousands of dollars, and occupying nearly all of Jeff's free time.

The process of renovation has borne fruit, however. One day Jeff salvaged a 15-foot *Lucky Strike* sign which he craftily installed above what was to become the Lanes' bar: a Dreamsicle-orange beauty, the sign is a gloried anachronism, especially when the Day-Glo paint blooms on the lanes during sessions of late night cosmic bowling.

Jeff has discovered other relics too, including a broadcast of good ol' *Mr. Rogers* filmed in the Lanes in the late '80s. According to Jeff, "We even found the ball he used in the intro!"

Despite the nifty brick-a-brack the renovation process has un-covered, Jeff's ultimate goal has always been providing for the Dormont community. That grocery store I mentioned? The Lanes' hosted a fund-raiser to help rebuild it. Elsewhere, Jeff brought in around $8,000 for a cancer benefit.

"We saved a little piece of this town," Jeff says, "It's only right to give back."

Jeff loves telling the story about one of Dormont's elderly res-idents returning to the Lanes: "This 88-year-old guy comes down and says, 'Oh my God, when I heard you were gonna reopen I prayed [that it was really happening]'." Turns out the guy used to be a pin boy at the Lanes in the '30s. And now he's home.

It's a striking story, and one that is indicative of a city on the rise again. Pittsburgh has always been a scrappy city, characterized by unflag-ging tenacity, even as outsourcing and the ills of globalization threatened its survival.

It's clear from Jeff's somewhat fading smile that even he's aware some of the community outreach focus has gotten in the way of turning any sort of serious profit. "Sometimes," he says, "I feel a bit like France bankrupting itself helping out the US."

There's clearly still a balance to finalize, but Jeff's been setting up more and more entertainment events to accomplish this. He becomes ecstatic again as he describes an upcoming event, "October 24th, man, there'll be a party with Danny Stagg, the lead guitarist from Kingdom Come…they used to tour with Metallica and Guns & Roses…[it'll be] '80s themed…and we want to make it an annual thing…'The Annual Head banger's Bowl!'"

From the glint in his eye, you can see Jeff's passion. He loves this city. The Lanes is a means of achieving a perfect symbiosis of community outreach and unabashed fun, despite the personal costs.

Jeff is confident he'll succeed. At the end of the Lane, he says, "Karma'll do its thing."

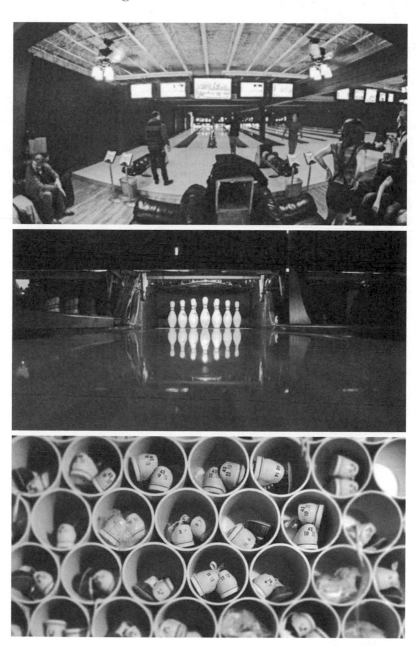

Images courtesy of Hollywood Lanes

The River Underneath the City

Scott Silsbe

I was half-drunk and exhausted and the bar
was loud with jukebox noise and Saturday drunks,
but I think I overheard Bob telling Moody about
the fourth river, the river underneath the city,
and about how the Mayans believe the point,
where the four rivers converge, to be a portal
that will take us all somewhere else later this year.

Just then the jukebox inexplicably ripped into
an old Dizzy Gillespie hard bop number,
which seemed to confuse and bewilder
a number of the people in the bar.
Five minutes into it, a woman shouted,
"Does anybody know how long this song is?"

I wondered how many people in the bar
knew about the river underneath the city.
It's strange how people can live somewhere
and not even know what is under their feet.
No stranger though than how we walk around
every day and don't know those around us.

It's funny how we think of each other but how
little we really know about each other. I didn't
know much more than the girl's name, but I can
still remember her at The Cage, can see her in
the booth, singing off-key along with the song
she played on the jukebox, "Greetings to the
New Brunette." I wonder if she's still in Chicago.

I'm Still a Jagov But I Love It

Scott Silsbe

We were at Take a Break, on the third level
where they keep the jukebox and the pool tables
when a guy said that, looking me in the eye
while he performed some twisted erotic dance
with a pool cue. He danced around to the other side
of the table and I sipped off my tall Yuengling
while he asked the woman he was playing,
"Am I the stripes or am I the other one?"

Bob Perkoski
Photographs

A Poem Written for the Aviary at a Time of its Possible Closing

Robert Gibb

Fabulous as the flowers
They preen among, the floating world
In which they come to rest

High in the hold of light,
They nest upon girders or wade
Through the waters of pools

Cloud-banked with shadows.
We find them choiring in branches,
In rookeries and dovecotes

Of the upturned ark of glass.
Because he has asked me,
I lift my young son up before

The condor's enormous darkness—
Its scruffy lei of feathers,
That head like a table scrap—

And feel his bones thrill
To be dangling there, fully
Within creation, as if heaven

Among us meant just such rooms.
Bernal Diaz thought as much,

Marching more than a mile into the sky

Above the New World,
Coming upon Tenochtitlan
Whose aviaries were brimming

With quetzals and macaws,
The hummingbirds, small jade
Blurs sipping nectars.

When Cortes burned the birds
Of paradise, their plumed flames
Drifted through the rubble

Of that sun, and the ashes
They would not be rising from,
Then or later, except as words

From this prayer spoken over water
In a place of wings
For creation's remnant flocks.

Steelworkers' Lockers, Pittsburgh History Center

Robert Gibb

The Forlornness of Metal they might as well
Be titled, these salvaged relics, props from a set
Long struck—the lap-welds and louvers
And green latch-locked doors bolted in line
In assembly, each the width of a man crammed in
Or hung in parts as in effigy. The bench hard
As a pew. Beyond, the mills were medieval,
Rows of stoves set four to the furnace, chimneys
In groves, hoists where they elevated the stock.

In the locker room, at the start of each shift,
Shucked aluminum suits got lowered on pulleys
From their ceiling roosts. We changed into
Forge-proof shoes, the hardhat's Day-Glo halo,
And stepped among flames, out into the annealing,
Where the world was turned to steel.

The Hall of Architecture

Robert Gibb

There in the past's attic, we stopped before
Plinths and entablatures, caryatids
Topped with their vast crowns, a pair of cupids
Bearing small stone wings: all of it hoarded
In that hall whose remnants we ranged among,
Dwarfed by portals and urns, the castings
Of the great doors of a baptistry
Where every panel disgorged its throng.
Even the radiators seemed monumental.
You found such maleness smothering, marble
And bronze being brunted by the will.
I remembered the mills when molten steel
Poured into molds, slag rose like coral reefs,
The scale of that labor now hard to conceive.

But then this was my house of wonders
While growing up—the horse of the sun
Surging from its stone, the horse of the moon
Setting—the great room's freight and plunder
As natural to me as the cliff wall
Rising along West Run Road, dates and names
Scrawled across its rocks. It was all the same:
The lettered bluff, the museum's sheer vaults
Carded from their quarry. This was Pittsburgh,
After all. I rode home on welded tracks,
Past open hearths and dark, purling rivers,
Buildings constructed out of granite blocks.
For me the past was an escarpment—
Something silent and shelfed and permanent.

Steel Engravings

Robert Gibb

1. Slag Banks

Nightly you'd see it, halfway up the sky,
That fissure of fire where the ladle cars
Tipped over, stoking the smoldering banks,
And below, where the glass of the river
Cast it back. Slag was what you were left with
When those fierce winds fled the ovens:

A breath hot as God's which melted metal,
Welled flux to the furnace top. Six times
A day they drew slag off—twice each shift—
To buckle in hills stark as stricken Isaiah.
You'd see it burning above Nine Mile Run
When the hinged cars clattered on the tracks.

In the beginning the planet cooled like that,
A mantle floating upon the molten core.
Slag was our horizon ringed with fire.

2. Steel Blooms

When ingots got lifted out of those pits
In which they'd been soaking up heat
And were broken, glowing, into sections,
One ton each, then we said steel had turned
Into blooms, the air about them flowering
Like light at the red end of the spectrum.

The whole mill seemed to be flourishing

Within the blush of that florescence
When we rolled them into rails: bright
Streaming ribbons, solid lengths of fire
We knew the world would soon travel
By twos over ties and gravel roadbeds.

Hot saw, we said, cutting lengths. Chill
And annealing. Grooving the mill, when it
All went well. Cupola and case and pulpit.

3. Pig Iron

Not, as I'd thought, owing to the crudeness
Of a metal fed with scrap, or because
It was rendered from the animal, the hocks
And hams compacted above its trotters,
The dark, gristly chambers of the heart.
And not because, like Latin, it was polyglot.

In the early furnaces they poured iron off
Into casting beds—each mold attached
To the other like pigs suckling at the sow.
Energy meant mass. Chimneys the size
Of brick-kilns, skips in which they charged
The stock. The belled dome of the hopper.

There were shifts when you were on the tit.
There were shifts when you did better
To remember the farrow eaten by their sow.

from The Employments of Time in Homestead

Robert Gibb

Because Fridays still mark the end of the week,
Whether there's work or not,

I head across the river to Chiodo's and listen
To lives whose dreams for the future

Fall to next year's teams. They waited here
For years for the mills to catch fire again,

Stacks massed like burning pillars,
For the sooty angels to ascend again

Into the furnaces of heaven. Waited
For the billowings of smoke from which

A still voice told them the dust had turned
To pollen, the iron been converted to steel,

There where slag heaps spilled their sunsets
From the lit rim of the world.

                    *

Today for my birthday my son gives me
The eight stapled pages of the book he's made

In which the boy plays baseball
And the father falls down, sweaty and tired,

At the end of a day of work. Shall I tell him
About the laid-off hosts I've sat with

Who would gladly collapse onto their bar-stools,
Rinsing the grit of metals from their throats

At the end of an eight-hour shift?
Or that I've found the only friend I grew up with

Who is still in town, and how, laboring
For Mesta until it closed, he spent

The next 10 years replacing windshields,
Too bitter to have sons of his own?

                    *

In a world where work is sacramental
Shall I tell him how, on those immense nights

Before inspection, I swept the mill floor clean
With powdered cement, eight hours

At union scale sowing that pale floury chaff
Until the floor shone softly as a granary's,

Or the milky surface of a mill pond in which
The moon was drowned, and how I'd pause,

Leaning on my broom as if it were a pole,
And what loomed above me weren't simply

Furnaces, but the actual machinery of heaven
In whose glory we were all employed.

Enclave

(for Jimmy Cvetic)

Matthew Plumb

The discipline inferred
in a basement level gym,
corner of Ross Street and Third,
builds worn gloves to rhythm
drum tight in the stitching
to the breathing, the bleeding.
Carried sweat and offal-sweet kit
a fusion of man thickening the air
same build of pressure and static
before arc
        of a strike
                out of nowhere.
You can angle testosterone
to the sway of a metronome,
speed bag and skipping rope,
acoustics of contact.
Out of nothing given, a taking back;
irony of forging the means to share.
A handing on of fire is a pact,
each potential ember brittle as hope.
Champions of their own lives
make the dimmest light thrive.

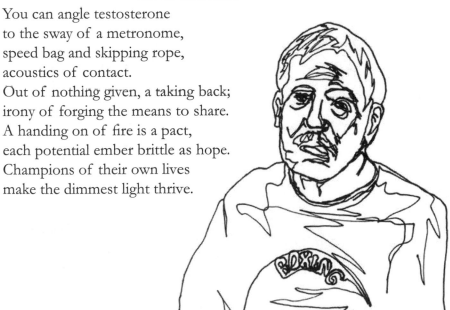

10¢

Shopping is your WARHOLIAN DUTY!

by Arielle Teer

EXITING THROUGH THE GIFT SHOP IS NOT SOMETHING ONLY BANKSY WOULD IMPLORE YOU TO DO, BUT I WOULD, TOO.

At The Andy Warhol Museum, or, colloquially *The Warhol*, you aren't forced to exit through the gift shop. In fact, you could just ride the elevator around and completely avoid it, or you could casually stroll past it upon your exiting stairway descent from the second floor. *But don't miss it! Make it a point to see it.*

Visit the gift shop. I implore you! The ghost of Andy Warhol, our Pope of Pop, implores you! Also, don't call it a gift shop. It is a store, for crying out loud, people. That isn't colloquial, that's practically a Holy Commandment.

Pop art is a joke that isn't a joke, and the melody of Bob Colacello repeats this to you from the first floor theater. It's hard to imagine a world where Warhol didn't mingle with the likes of Bob Colacello, Lou Reed, Edie Sedgwick, Keith Haring, and Jean-Michel Basquiat— and that's just to vastly under-qualify the networking prowess of Warhol.

But long before he was Warhol, he was actually Warhola.

Andrew Warhola was born in 1928 in Pittsburgh to Carpatho-Rusyn immigrants. He was the youngest of three, with two brothers named Paul and John. His father, Andrej Warhola, died when Warhol was only 14, but saved enough to send his youngest to college. Andrej told John to make sure Andy went to school. Little Andy was going to be somebody. Early on, he knew it. He believed in him.

Growing up, Warhol visited the local cinema, watched Shirley Temple on TV, and experimented with his own film in the basement. He graduated from Schenley High. Afterwards, he attended Carnegie Institute of Technology, which is now Carnegie Mellon University, where he studied commercial art. Did you know he almost failed? *Almost.* After graduating, he moved to the Big Apple and the rest is, as they say, history.

M'MM, CAN'T YOU SMELL THAT SWEET PURSUIT OF THE AMERICAN DREAM?

To neglect the influence and help of Warhol's family in his success would be remiss. His mother, Julia, moved to New York City in 1951 to live with him. She sang folk songs, made tin flowers, and even illustrated alongside him. Her favorite subjects were cats and angels, while her son's were celebrities and soup cans. Warhol was nonchalantly American in his humble roots and relentless pursuit of glamour. He carefully crafted his enigmatic persona of business executive, band manager, commercial artist, and provocateur. Warhol was completely Pittsburgh in the way Halston jokingly called him "the coal miner's daughter," perhaps a nod to his own midwest roots. Did you know Warhol almost died twice? *Almost.* In 1968, Warhol was shot by Valerie Solanas, which left him scarred. Sadly, Warhol died in the plainest of terms during a routine gallbladder surgery in 1987.

Yes, the store is my favorite part of the museum, but not just because of commerce. It was this Prince of Pop who wrote:

"I WOULD RATHER WATCH SOMEBODY BUY THEIR UNDERWEAR THAN READ A BOOK THEY WROTE."

Luckily for you, dear future shopper, we don't sell underwear. But that's me behind the counter, winking at you. The store is a place where you can unbutton your collar (*no matter the color*) and shop. Shopping is for everyone. Start your own collection like Warhol's time capsules. Browse the front windows and view emerging artists in the *Exposures* series, an homage to Warhol's early career in creating window displays for places like Horne's Department Store in Pittsburgh. You should walk across the 7th Street bridge, the Andy Warhol Bridge, to get to the museum. It's the same bridge he walked on. If you're so inclined, you can even make your dutiful pilgrimage to St. John the Baptist Byzantine Catholic Cemetery in Bethel Park to see the grave of Andy Warhol. *But do remember*, as you peruse the quirky, kitschy, and funny mix of store supplies that Warhol also said:

"WHEN YOU THINK ABOUT IT, DEPARTMENT STORES ARE KIND OF LIKE MUSEUMS."

BUY NOW!

Contributors

Bethany Lang is a Pittsburgh native, born and raised in the South Hills. She currently works as a nonprofit software trainer in Chicago. Her website is BethanyLang.com.

Jody DiPerna grew up just outside Pittsburgh in the shadow of the Allegheny Ludlum Steel Mill in Brackenridge, Pennsylvania. She has written for several national websites, as well as multiple Pittsburgh outlets, including *City Paper*, the *Tribune-Review*, *Table* and *Pittsburgh Quarterly*. She spent an entire year following around a barn-storming women's football team, survived more nights on the sidelines of high school football fields than she would care to admit, and conducted one of her finest interviews in a laundromat.

Nico Chiodi is fifteen years old, homeschooled, and has lived in Pittsburgh all his life. He started singing with the PBC at age four and transitioned to playing banjo at age 7. He also now plays with his dad and brother all around the city as *The Chiodi Trio*, who can be seen most weekends in the summer in front of Wholey's Fish Market in the Strip. Besides playing the 4-string banjo, he writes, mostly fiction, reads, and plays board games.

Sean Posey has spent the last several years photographing the landscape and researching the history of the Pittsburgh area. Both a photographer and an urban historian, he is currently working on a book entitled *Lost Youngstown*, which will be published in 2016 by the History Press. His work can be viewed at SeanPoseyphoto.photoshelter.com

Brendan Hykes grew up in Turtle Creek, just outside of Pittsburgh, and has lived in the PGH area his whole life. He has had a passion for writing since childhood, in all genres, formats and styles. More of his work can be found at BrendanHykes.tumblr.com.

Chris "Chance!" Brown is PGH's Favorite Overstayed Journeyman Cartoonist. A freelance and studio animator, illustrator and storyboardist, Brown has been working on shorts and comic pieces for the past seven years and is currently developing pitches for *Metal Hurlant* and *2000AD*.

Cody McDevitt is an award-winning journalist currently working full-time for the *Somerset Daily American*, a small newspaper outside of Pittsburgh. His work has appeared in numerous publications, including *Men's Journal* and the *Pittsburgh Post-Gazette*.

Jess Craig is a senior at the University of Pittsburgh pursuing dual degrees: a BS in Microbiology and a BA in English writing. She is the Editor-in-Chief of the creative science magazine, *The Pitt Pulse*, and is a former opinions columnist for *The Pitt News*. Jess has published nonfiction essays in *A&U Magazine* and *WomanScope News Magazine*.

Rachel Wilkinson has an MFA in nonfiction from the University of Pittsburgh. Her essays appear in *Identity Theory*, *The Atlas Review*, and *Green Briar Review*.

Kyle Mimnaugh moved to Pittsburgh in 2013. He is a lover of film and television, science fiction, and coffee. He is guaranteed to be the most morose person you will ever meet.

Robert Yune transferred to the University of Pittsburgh in 2001 and has been living in the Burgh ever since. "Time Capsule, 2005" is an excerpt from his first book, *EIGHTY DAYS OF SUNLIGHT* (Thought Catalog Books/Prospecta Press), published in 2015. His website is RobertYune.com.

J.J. Lendl is a native Pittsburgher who was raised in Beechview, lives in Shadyside, and is fluent in Pittsburghese. Along with his work in writing and graphic arts, he is also a filmmaker, actor, and musician. You can check out more of his artwork at Xfilesposterproject.tumblr.com.

Adam Dupaski lived in Pittsburgh for a spell after college. Originally from Ohio, he now lives in Kraków, Poland. His work has appeared in *Plotki*, *Right-Hand Pointing*, and *The Appalachian School*. More of his writing can be found at Lethatechnique.wordpress.com.

Andy Kohler spent time in Pittsburgh while in a rock band. He recently quit his day job to write full-time. You can connect with him on Twitter at @AndyKohler1.

Melanie Cox McCluskey was born and raised in Pittsburgh and is the managing editor of *Pop City Media*, as well as a former beat reporter for the *Pittsburgh Tribune-Review*. Her work has appeared in *The Philadelphia Inquirer*, *Pittsburgh Business Quarterly*, *NEXT Pittsburgh*, *Venus Zine*, and *Maniac Magazine*. Read more at MelanieCoxMcCluskey.com

Ben Gwin was raised in New Jersey but moved to Pittsburgh in 2001, and currently lives in Bloomfield with his daughter. Ben's fiction has appeared or is forthcoming in, *The Normal School, Word Riot, Mary: A Journal of New Writing*, and others. His novel manuscript, *Clean Time: The True Story of Ronald Reagan Middleton*, was shortlisted for the 2014 Pressgang Prize. He is the Fiction Editor at Burrow Press Review.

Rebecca Morgan is a painter and ceramics artist from the mountains of central Pennsylvania. Her artwork focuses on the rural woods of western PA and people who live there. Morgan holds an MFA from the Pratt Institute and is represented by the Asya Geisberg Gallery in New York. Her website is RebeccaMorganart.com

Amy Jo Burns grew up in a small town about halfway between Pittsburgh and Erie. She's the author of Cinderland, a Rust Belt memoir of fire, steel, and long held secrets. You can find her on Twitter at @amyjoburns.

Eric Boyd is the editor of this collection. He has lived in and around Pittsburgh most of his life and is currently writing a short story collection based in Homestead, PA, called *Brownfields*. His writing has appeared in, among others, *Prison Noir* (Akashic Books), *Words Without Walls* (Trinity University Press) *Guernica*, *The Offing magazine*, *PEN America Journal*, and *Fourth River*. His blog is over at EricBoydblog.tumblr.com.

LaToya Ruby Frazier (born 1982, Braddock, Pennsylvania) works in photography, video and performance to build visual archives that address industrialism, rustbelt revitalization, environmental justice, healthcare inequity, family and communal history. In 2015 her first book *The Notion of Family* (Aperture 2014) received the International Center for Photography Infinity Award.

Matthew Newton is a writer and editor from Western Pennsylvania, where he lives in the Electric Valley with his wife and two young sons. His essays have been published by *Oxford American*, *Guernica*, *The Rumpus*, and *The Morning News*; his reporting has appeared in *Esquire*, *Forbes*, and *Spin*. He is currently at work on *Shopping Mall*, his first book, which will be published by Bloomsbury in fall 2016. For more information, visit MatthewNewton.us.

Yona Harvey is the author of the poetry collection, *Hemming the Water*, winner of the Kate Tufts Discovery Award. Her work has appeared in many publications; most recently, *The Volta Book of Poets*. She is an assistant professor in the University of Pittsburgh Writing Program.

Mauricio Kilwein Guevara was born in Belencito, Colombia in 1961 and came with his family to Pittsburgh (Hazelwood, Library, Bethel Park) as a small child. He is the author of four volumes of poetry, most recently *POEMA* (University of Arizona Press), one book of translations published in Spain, one play with a staged reading Off-Broadway, and is currently finishing a novel set primarily in Ecuador. Check out his poem "Rhyme for Halloween" at the Poetry Foundation website: PoetryFoundation.org/poem/247394.

Dave Newman was born in the old Clark candy bar factory on Pittsburgh's North Shore, in the infirmary, where his grandfather worked and where his mother, 9-months pregnant, stopped by to deliver lunch. He is the author of five books, including *The Poem Factory* (White Gorilla Press, 2015), the novel *Two Small Birds* (Writers Tribe Books, 2014), and the collection *The Slaughterhouse Poems* (White Gorilla Press, 2013), named one of the best books of the year by L Magazine. He lives in Trafford, PA, the last town in the Electric Valley, with his wife, the writer Lori Jakiela, and their two children.

John Lawson teaches writing and rhetoric at Robert Morris University in Pittsburgh. His poems and plays have been published in numerous print and online venues including *Main Street Rag, Paper Street*, and *Uppagus*. His poetry chapbook, *Generations*, was published by St. Andrews University Press in 2007.

Terrance Hayes is a poet and educator who has published five poetry collections. His 2010 collection, *Lighthead*, won the National Book Award for Poetry in 2010, and in September 2014 he was a recipient of the prestigious MacArthur fellowship. His latest book is *How to be Drawn* (Penguin). His website is TerranceHayes.com

Lori Jakiela grew up in Trafford, Pennsylvania where she worked Bingo nights at the Trafford Polish Hall. She is the author of three memoirs—*Miss New York Has Everything; The Bridge to Take When Things Get Serious*; and *Belief Is Its Own Kind of Truth, Maybe*—as well as a poetry collection, *Spot the Terrorist*. For more, visit LoriJakiela.net.

Rachel Mabe moved to Pittsburgh in the summer of 2014 and has enjoyed getting to know the city on foot. Mabe is a graduate student in Pitt's MFA program (nonfiction); she also teaches writing at the university, and interns for the Longform podcast. Learn more at RachelMabe.com.

Michael Gerhard Martin was raised in rural Pennsylvania and lived in Pittsburgh for 14 years. His first book, *Easiest If I Had A Gun*, was a finalist for the Iowa prize, and his short story about homophobia, bullying, and gun violence, "Shit Weasel Is Late For Class," won the 2013 James Knudsen Prize for fiction from the University of New Orleans and Bayou Magazine. Like him at Facebook.com/MichaelGerhardMartin.

Ann Curran, a Pittsburgh native, lives on Mount Washington. She's author of *Placement Test* and *Me First*, the latter described by Samuel Hazo, founder of the International Poetry Forum, as "a book like no other...a poetry of utter frankness...as unignorable as it is rare." She is a member of the Squirrel Hill Poetry Workshop. You can reach her at AnnCurran@comcast.net.

Lisa Toboz is a photographer and writer working primarily with Polaroid film. Her photography has appeared in *Blur Magazine*, *Poladarium*, *Pryme Magazine*, and *Optiko*. A native Pittsburgher, she now lives in the Garfield neighborhood with her husband, artist Jeff Schreckengost. Find out more at LisaToboz.squarespace.com.

Kevin Tasker is a native Clevelander with a Pittsburgh fetish. He's reported on Tamir Rice and Cavs culture for *Belt*, reviewed yogurt for *McSweeney's*, visited white collar madness for *SCENE*, and dashed off a few small things on love / bikes for *Thought Catalog*.

Scott Silsbe was born in Detroit, but now lives in Pittsburgh where he writes, sells books, and makes music with friends. His poems have appeared in numerous print and web periodicals including *Chiron Review*, *Nerve Cowboy*, *The Chariton Review*, *Third Coast*, *The Volta*, and *The Cultural Weekly*. He is the author of two poetry collections: *Unattended Fire* (Six Gallery Press, 2012) and *The River Underneath the City* (Low Ghost Press, 2013).

Bob Perkoski moved to PGH in 1975 to attend art school at The Ivy School of Professional Art, where he majored in Photography; he returned to Ohio around 1979. Currently he is a freelance photographer in Cleveland shooting regularly for *Belt* and *Fresh Water Cleveland*, where he is managing photographer. Previously he was co-founder/publisher/photographer/graphic designer for *Balanced Living Magazine*, a printed mag distributed around the Cleveland area featuring holistic living, environmentalism and personal growth. See more at Perkoski.com

Robert Gibb was born in the steel town of Homestead, Pennsylvania. He is the author of ten books of poetry, including *The Origins of Evening*, which was a National Poetry Series winner. Among his other awards are two National Endowment for the Arts Grants, seven Pennsylvania Council on the Arts grants, a Pushcart Prize, the Camden Poetry Award, The Wildwood Poetry Prize, and the Devil's Millhopper Chapbook Prize. He currently lives on New Homestead Hill above the Monongahela River.

Matthew Plumb's love of libraries brought him to discovering Pittsburgh, the place where the free public library was born. Coming from South Wales, whose valley towns are haunted by the ghosts of industrialisation, Plumb feels an affinity to Pittsburghers and their ability to forge on. His blog is Plumbpoetry.blogspot.co.uk.

Robert Qualters is an American painter, installation artist and printmaker based in Pittsburgh. He has completed more than two-dozen public murals and site-specific installations and his work is represented in the permanent collections of the Carnegie Museum of Art; the Oakland California Museum of Art; and the Westmoreland County Museum of Art in Greensburg, Pennsylvania. In 2014 he was named the Pennsylvania Artist of the Year. His website is Qualtersart.com.

Arielle Teer lives in Pittsburgh and is currently working on a project about her peacenik aunt. View more of her work at ArielleTeer.com.

Dave DiCello is a photographer born and raised in Pittsburgh. His photography has appeared in *Pittsburgh Magazine*, *Landmarks Magazine*, *Western Pennsylvania Magazine*, and *Lonely Planet Travel Magazine*. He has also worked with The Pittsburgh Penguins, Pitt Panthers, Duquesne University, and the Pittsburgh Cultural Trust. His website is DaveDiCello.com

Editor's Acknowledgements

T*his book would not have been possible* without the incredible support Belt provided me. Anne Trubek and Anna Clark were enthusiastic throughout the submission and editing process, even when I'm convinced I was wearing on their patience.

Once the manuscript was compiled I had the unbelievable honor to work with Chelsea Leber and Zoe Gould, two copywriters/proofreaders who saved my ass more than a few times when I had ridiculous ideas or notes. This book is only as polished and professional as they made it; without them, I'd probably still be drafting with people and asking Belt for one more month, one more month, one more month. And our designer, Haley Stone, whose previous work with Belt has been stunning, continued her good work with this book, including the design of the book's amazing cover, which features a photo from Dave DiCello. I asked DiCello to create an image of the iconic Pittsburgh Point, where the three rivers meet--but I wanted to see it in a new way. Dave delivered, and anyone picking up this book will see its fresh perspective right from the very start because of his work. I'm also indebted to Michelle Blankenship, whose help with this book will no doubt be a huge factor in its success. I am also grateful for the support for this book's publication provided by the Carnegie Museum of Art.

Of course my family and friends stuck behind me and I'd be lost without them. In particular I'm grateful to Brian Morgan, an MFA classmate who directed me to Belt in the first place. Also my good colleague and friend Oscar, whose tireless support often amounted to his waking me up at 3AM to keep reading/editing. All of you folks who pushed me by asking, "How's the book coming?" when I was too worn out to work on it, thanks.

However, none of this would matter without the amazing writers and artists in this collection. Had it been possible, this book would have been 1000 pages long, that's how many good submissions came in; still, I'm more than satisfied with what we've put together. Yinz are alright with me.